Tales of a Rock Star's Daughter

Nettie Baker

Tales of a Rock Star's Daughter

Nettie Baker

WP
WYMER
PUBLISHING
Bedford, England

First published in Great Britain in 2018
by Wymer Publishing
Bedford, England
www.wymerpublishing.co.uk
Tel: 01234 326691
Wymer Publishing is a trading name of Wymer (UK) Ltd

ISBN 978-1-912782-02-4

Edited by Jerry Bloom.

Typeset by The Andys
Printed and bound in Great Britain by
Clays Ltd, Bungay, Suffolk

A catalogue record for this book is available from the British Library.

Cover design by The Andys.
Cover photos © Nettie Baker.

PART ONE
'TEACH YOUR CHILDREN WELL'
1974 - 84

'Time like an ever rolling stream bears all its sons away, they fly forgotten as a dream dies at the opening day.'
('Oh God Our Help in Ages Past': Isaac Watts, Traditional Hymn)

CONTENTS

CHAPTER ONE
Maida Vale: 1974

Shafts of sunlight played along the broad sweep of Elgin Avenue. Tall London plane trees shook their new green leaves coquettishly in defiance at the previous year's pendulous old seeds, left jangling on the branches like a barmaid's earrings. It was a Friday afternoon in the middle of May and we were experiencing one of those sudden bursts of premature summer that has Londoners lolling about in parks during their lunch hour and casting off their clothes with gay abandon.

The Edgware road was full of traffic. Hillman Avengers, Humbers, Hunters, Huskies, Imps, Minx's, Sunbeams and Supersnipes. Ford Anglias, Escorts, Capris, Consuls, Cortinas, Zodiacs and Zephyrs. Transit vans jostling with Commas, Bedfords and HA Vivas. Heavy goods vehicles, black taxis and removal vans; Austin Allegros, 1100s, 1800s and Cambridges all vying for space with Triumphs, Rovers, little A35s, Morris Oxfords, Rileys, Wolsey 16/60s, Marinas, Minors, Travellers and Mini Clubmans. A foreign contingent of VW Beetles and Camper Vans, odd shaped BMWs, Scimitars, Lancias, Datsuns, Fiats, Renaults and Citroens alongside bulky Mercs and Saabs. A noisy jam of flashing chrome, honking horns, screeching brakes and revving engines.Hot with the fumes of leaded petrol and heavy with the carbon emissions of unregulated diesel exhausts.

There goes a Cooper S cutting up some poor bastard in a Vauxhall Viva whose irate driver is now sandwiched at the lights between a Jag and a Jensen Healey. Further along past the junction some bloke in an MG tries his luck with a blonde in a bright yellow Frogeye Sprite, nearly colliding with a dark blue Range Rover in the process. In the midst of all this mundane confusion comes a number thirteen Routemaster bus. Its dusty paintwork glaring brick red in the sun as it trundles slowly along, swaying slightly, with the conductor hanging nonchalantly off the back platform like a gypsy on a fairground ride.

The bus lurches to a halt at Maida Vale. Two girls emerge from the top deck. They are the same age as the number of the bus and they crash down the twisting steps in an ungainly fashion wearing skyscraper platform shoes. Then they come to rest in a less than dignified heap on the gritty pavement. The conductor laughs, the bus groans and sets off down the Edgware Road towards Marble Arch. The afternoon shimmers in the heat.

The two girls stagger back and survey the wreckage at their feet with a jaundiced dismay. They are dressed in white shirts and pleated grey skirts that have been rolled up ridiculously short. A couple of splitting carrier bags are filled with never to be attempted homework, whilst another is crammed with clothes. A paper back of Jane Austen's 'Northanger Abbey' lies face down in the sticky spillage of a coke bottle, its pages being perused in a desultory manner by unseen fingers. One girl prods at it with the toe of her cream, pearlised Lilley & Skinner's platform sandal and discusses with her companion the merits of condemning what was in their opinion the world's most boring book (along with Thomas Hardy's 'Return of the Native') to an ignominious and littery grave. The prettier of the two casts her shadow over the prostrate tome and her long dark hair blows across her face. She smiles a dazzler and she has a large mouth, perfect white teeth, brown eyes and personality. After some further banter, the book is stuffed back into the carrier bag with the most room and the least splits. They stand up and even out their loads, holding the bulky bags across their chests. The sun winks off the silver wing mirrors and bumpers of the passing vehicles as they dodge perilously through the traffic and run off down the hill laughing.

* * *

Now you may or may not have guessed that the not as pretty girl was me. The other one was Louise (now the singer & actress Louise English) and Louise lived in Elgin Avenue. This wide thoroughfare showed off great blocks of graceful red brick Victorian apartments. They had long hallways from which all the rooms opened and magnificent living spaces that overlooked the plane trees whose waving branches afforded odd glimpses of the passers by on the street below.

Louise lived in Ashworth Mansions and her flat also boasted a little balcony on which often sat a fat black and tan sausage dog called 'Patch'. In the living room hung a large portrait of a glamorous blonde in a sparkly black dress, gazing wistfully and seductively out of the frame. That was Louise's mum. She was a singer with a voice that could blow the roof off and as my Dad often remarked, she was additionally gifted with, 'a fine pair'. The portrait left a lasting impression on me. I related to the concept that you could be forever captured in some fairytale moment outside of time and that a dressed up and idealised version of yourself could look down from the wall at your disappointing future and remind you of your hopeful past.

'I must get one', I thought.

I was staying at Louise's for the weekend. Nowadays, they use the Americanism 'sleepover', what sort of tosh is that? We had never heard the word, but we had heard the word 'party' which is what we planned to hold on the Saturday night. We would invite everyone from school (not many, as there were only about six in our class) and as many boys as we could find (again not many).

Louise had a friend, Amanda Davies, who lived nearby and Amanda had a brother named Miles. Miles Davies — this made my mother laugh for now obvious reasons, but I have to confess that at the time I never knew what the bloody hell she was going on about. Our Miles however, did not play the trumpet and was a God on legs. There definitely was 'miles and miles of Miles' (one of my lame attempts at humour), because he was immensely tall and gangly. His face was very Jim Morrison, with a square jaw framed by curls, which in his case were blond. How beautiful he was, someone whom I had the privilege to snog (you know, tongues) now and again during our many enjoyable games of Spin the Bottle.

Louise also had a brother Clive, who was a year or two older than us and he was witty and pretty with deep brown eyes. In addition to these accomplishments, he could also play Beatles tunes on the piano and Beach Boys songs on the guitar. As he sang, my friends and I would sigh softly and gaze at his face in rapt attention.

'*Barbara Ann, I wanna hold your hand....*'

The boys also had a few friends here and there, but mostly 'there' because they went to 'Woolverstone Hall,' a boy's boarding school in Ipswich. A group of us girls had once travelled all the way to Ipswich by train to see them and when we got there we sat out in their school playing field in the sun. Then we sang all the way home, hardly noticing the burrs that were still stuck to our clothes and the stray blades of grass in our pockets. We 'girls' attended a private school in the Finchley Road, hence the ride to Elgin Avenue on the number thirteen bus.

Our school was a ballet school and this meant that rather than do any PE at all we did about four hours of classical ballet a day instead. Classmate Anita was very good at this indeed and it was a shame for her that she was far too short to ever be given work as a ballerina. The rest of us possessed varying degrees of talent. Sheryl had amazingly high insteps that looked impressive, but they caused her to break the backs of her pointed shoes and she had to have them reinforced with extra steel inserts. Louise and I could never do *Adage*, (the slow bit with your legs round your ears) and we'd often fall over and get the giggles in class.

All this high powered dancing and prancing about would lead up to the school show that was held in July every year, at the Golden Lane Theatre, Barbican. So towards the end of the summer term we could be seen trolling purposefully about the underground stations of Barbican, Farringdon and Moorgate, armed with bags full of pointed shoes and tutus as we marched off for endless dress rehearsals.

These shows of ours often got quite unintentionally dramatic. During one ballet that had been entitled 'Invitation to the Dance', in which we all wore purple tutus; Miranda and Dinah collided on stage doing posé turns from opposite corners. This was rather like a badly coordinated Red Arrows stunt and they left the stage limping and in tears, trailing the wreckage of their costumes behind them. Dinah, when she was starring as the eponymous hero in 'Peter and the Wolf', knocked the scenery over and all of us (who were watching in the wings) cracked up including Dinah who was in full view of the audience. Consequently she got a rollicking for her 'unprofessional' behaviour.

On another occasion, Louise had been cast as Red Riding Hood and I was playing the part of her mother. We had an affectionate dance routine to execute convincingly, but Louise, whilst smiling benignly at the audience, viciously demanded that I keep away from her because she perhaps quite understandably felt concerned that I might infect her with my Chicken Pox, the spots of which had come out that very day. This was rather difficult for me to achieve. When we gambolled about as two of Snow White's dwarves, she again got well narky with me because I accidentally pulled her hat off every time the choreography called upon me to restrain her. Lastly, a splendid Polish dance known as 'Krakoviac', ended with a grand finale in which Louise found herself unable to re-enter the circle of happy skipping friends, whose hands were clasped tightly against her. 'Let me in, let me in!' She begged, as we whirled merrily around in fits of stifled laughter.

Of course our school was the place where the first steps to these marvellous dances were put together. It was known as The Stella Mann School of Dancing and had been named for its founder (a martinet indeed and a survivor of the horrors of German occupation in Europe). It was situated on the Finchley Road, just up past Frognal station, in a very tall Victorian building whose lower reaches comprised of the Alan Day Mercedes garage. Two large dance studios sat above this showroom and the rest of the classrooms, dressing rooms and other obscure places, such as a secret leotard making factory, could be reached by going up and down several flights of cold, grey lino covered stairs.

The main dressing room had a row of metal lockers against one wall and there were several benches and chairs draped with wet towels and various pieces of ballet related clothing (one such ultra stretchy item was somewhat alarmingly known as a 'Jock Belt'). In this room the tears and tribulations of the terribly bitchy world of ballet were played out; mainly by the older students who were working towards their Intermediate or Advanced RAD examinations and who lived on vast quantities of black coffee and cigarettes.

At the foot of the middle staircase, adjacent to a gloomy bathroom, a drinks machine was one day installed and we were very excited indeed by the prospect. However, tea, coffee, hot chocolate, unspecified soup and a drink named 'orange juice' (yet bearing no relation to it) often came out on their own without the cup and/or the water, much to our surprise.

The building was full of twists and turns and endless dark stairways surmounted by tall windows that looked out over the sea of rooftops that sailed away to the hazy distances of Swiss Cottage and Kilburn. Not surprising then, that with all this and teenaged girls too, things could get creepy. One night when we were staying late for ballet, Louise converted the top of a wooden desk into an Ouija Board. She carefully drew the letters on with chalk and used the plastic cup off a thermos flask as a pointer. Bloody hell, it scared the life out of me because it did move on its own. But then we decided Louise had been pushing it, so we tried it again when she'd gone home and it really did seem to be going for it. That scared me more. As a result, we kept on with it until we believed that we had made contact with a fifteenth-century monk called Hans. Then we saw ghosts in the toilets and the teachers went funny and the room spun round and my mum said, 'Bloody stop doing that now will you'.

So we did and we all came to school with crosses on chains round our necks for ages afterwards!

When we had first started at the school in the early 70's we were taught by an old man. He took us for Maths, History and Geography and his name was Mr Coulson. He was a good teacher and we were terrified of him, mainly because he thought we were all inordinately stupid and he wasn't shy about telling us. He regularly got so annoyed and red in the face during lessons that he would have to loosen his tie and go and stand by the open window to cool down. He would often sit at his desk and lay out a handkerchief, then he would set about methodically cutting up an apple with a fruit knife, which he would go on to consume noisily as he explained to us important facts about the Saxons and Welshmen making Coracles. But before long he got cross again and apples would go flying everywhere as he shouted at us 'Donkeys.'

'Teaching you lot is like getting a horse that's been dead for twenty years and telling it to get up and run.' This was accompanied by the actions of him whipping the top of his desk in an attitude of genuine despair. My maths book was filled entirely with large red crosses and during a heated explanation of some simple equation that I totally failed to master, he once said to me, 'In all my forty-five years of teaching, I have NEVER met a girl like you!'

A compliment indeed, though I don't think he meant it that way. Finally, and probably mercifully for him, he retired and we bought him a crystal decanter and a huge card with a picture of a donkey on the front.

After Mr Coulson we got Mr Milestone and we were not remotely scared of this poor bloke. His name in truth was Mr Millston, but however much he went mad and said he was NOT Mr Milestone, Mr Milestone he remained. He was obviously newly married and he often mentioned his wife, so we mentioned his wife a lot as well. We were studying Metternich and Windisch-Grätz, the Austrians being revolting and the empire being on the brink of collapse when a hilarious girl called Debbie London fell off her chair and told us helpfully that she was also on, 'the brink of collapse'. Mr Milestone berated Debbie for not looking at him whilst he was speaking. After some time Debbie put up her hand.

'Mr Milestone?'

'Yes Debbie?'

'My Dad says that you listen with your ears, not your eyes.'

Shrieks of mirth followed this sage announcement and this is the sort of thing that poor Mr Milestone had to suffer day in and day out at our hands. I can't understand why it was that we all failed our History O'level, but all I can remember of the syllabus is that Charlotte Corday stabbed Marat in his bath and Castlereagh slit his own throat with a razor. Oh and Mr Milestone chasing me down the stairs with a board rubber as I waved him on and taunted, 'Come on, hit me then.' I secretly taped one lesson in order to alert our parents to how useless our teachers were. After listening in silence for some minutes my Dad said, 'And I'm paying £250 a term for that.'

Where all the other parents got this kind of money from I have no idea, except that for Louise and I it appeared to be the proceeds of 'showbiz'. Where her Dad (classical musician Anthony English) was I don't know either, she did tell me but I've forgotten (this is called having little interest in vital information). However, her Mum shared the apartment in Ashworth Mansions with a handsome and younger bloke called Michael.

In that sweltering May of 1974, our plan for Saturday daytime was to find boys for Saturday nighttime. Party day dawned as hot as ever and we trawled Elgin Avenue in the heat perfecting our plan, and buying stuff for the evening. Then we retired to Louise's white, chiffon-draped bedroom (that was heavily papered with posters of David Cassidy) to compose a letter to a boy across the way who was called something dashing like Stephen Barcway. A letter was duly posted through the door of this poor boy. He did reply, but in an extremely obscure fashion, which indicated that he was a bit worried about being stalked and anyway was far too gorgeous for the likes of us. Nevertheless, we were encouraged.

Soon enough the shadows began to lengthen into a light and fragrant evening. We'd got our supplies of Cinzano and lemonade and our multi-coloured, gold-tipped Balkan Sobranie cigarettes. Where on earth did we get them? We *always* had them and never mind if you choked to death (because they were really strong), you could match them to your outfit; that was the point dears. We took ages getting ready, but finally we were and I gazed at myself in the wide living room mirror, admiring my skinny sunburnt arms that extended from a green and lilac Lurex tank top.

Guests began to arrive and who were they? A boy with large dark glasses and stubbly short brown hair, remembered only as 'The Mole'. Anita and Sheryl from school, Amanda and various other girls from the vicinity attired in huge great platform wedge shoes and calf-length A-line skirts with embroidered pockets. So many of the girls at this time seemed to us to go by the names of 'Lyn' or 'Mary' that we used the term '*Lyn Mary*' to allude to those that we judged as being a bit, well, common. Not that Amanda was one of them, but she did have other notable attributes. My mum for one was always amazed at the size of her DD chest compared to the rest of us who were still as flat as ironing boards. Tall and/or busty were plus points to us when it came to buying booze and getting tickets for X films, and I was tall. Often Louise and Anita, who were short, would just get behind me at the counter and push, whilst 'Fonz' here (as I liked to call myself), always got the goods. Amanda's brother Miles arrived fashionably late to the strains of Carly Simon's 'You're so Vain.' *'You had one eye in the mirror as you watched yourself go by.'* Louise said it was the right song for him.

Now we settled down to play 'Spin the Bottle' and what a brilliant game that is. You sit in a circle, spin an empty bottle and if it points to a member of the opposite sex who you aren't related to then off you go! Ah, I never tired of that game, beats bloody Postman's Knock into a cocked hat any day. Due to the shortage of young males, there was inevitably a bit of rivalry regarding the limited stocks available. Miles and Clive must have had a high old time being passed around amongst the 'Stella's' girls, with poor Amanda and Louise having even less choice than the rest of us. I for one (and I was not alone in this), had massive crushes on both of them at some point, but Miles with his tall beauty, was the one that I loved the best.

So there we were, spinning the bottle, drinking our Cinzano, coughing away on our Balkan Sobranies and bopping about to Elton John, Slade, Gary Glitter (not excusing his then unknown crimes, but the music was part of life in those days), T-Rex, Mud, Sweet, The Osmonds and The Jackson Five. I had bought Elton's 'Goodbye Yellow Brick Road' double LP at the first opportunity and Bernie Taupin's lyrics taught many of us more about life than perhaps he ever intended as we listened wide eyed to songs that dealt with subjects such as lesbianism and prostitution.

Later, we would find ourselves slow dancing the night away to David Cassidy ballads with whatever boy(s) we were lucky enough to strike up a rapport with for the evening. Or we might end up in a huddle with the girls, giving dirty looks to some brazen outsider (didn't the boys always go for them?), and/or rushing sobbing to the toilet when we noticed the object of our desire trying to get his hand up said *Lyn Mary's* cheesecloth shirt.

Darkness came dropping softly like one of the gas shells in Wilfred Owen's 'Dulce et Decorum Est' (we were doing it for O' level), though thankfully not with the same result. Some of us wandered out onto the balcony and breathed deeply of the petrol-tainted air, warm and suburban. Then we called out encouragement as a P6 Rover overtook a Triumph Herald with a scrunch of syncromesh and went roaring off up the street. Eventually, the Cinzano had all been drunk and youngsters began to stagger away in small groups. When everyone had gone, Louise, Anita, Sheryl and I pulled on our nightdresses, got into our camp beds in Louise's room and dissected the evening. One by one we drifted off to sleep as David Cassidy stared impassively down upon us from his place near the ceiling. Outside, the 1974 stars twinkled over Maida Vale. Street lights winked amongst the rustling leaves of the tall London Planes and the teenagers to whom not much had happened yet, dreamed hopefully on, ready for more adventurers.

CHAPTER TWO
The Rainbow: February, 1975

A drunken scrawl in my tiny diary proclaims *'I'm in the Rainbow Theatre! 'We've just been backstage! Ni (Anita) is here somewhere. Jap, me & Mum, Nanny & Grandad are in front. Lee has just been really nice to me!'* It continues thus and then trails off with a heart. The explanation for such high spirits is that my father was by this time playing with Paul and Adrian Gurvitz in The Baker Gurvitz Army. This was a change of direction and uniform from his Ginger Baker's Airforce and quite appropriate because in the latter they were all high and flying and in the former they were mostly having a ruck.

'Jap' was Janet Mary Pritchard, my best friend to end all best friends and I'd met her when we'd hit the big time with Cream and moved from our one-bedroom maisonette in Neasden, to a four-bedroom detached house at the bottom of Harrow-On-The Hill. Up until then I'd had to share a bedroom with Mum and Dad, but then in the February of 1968, my sister Leda had been born, so things were getting a bit over crowded to say the least. We hadn't moved before that time, because for the previous two years Dad had been almost constantly on tour with Cream. In fact, on the bleak morning that Leda burst into the world, Dad's mother (who was staying with us for the birth) telephoned him at his hotel room in the States. 'You have a beautiful baby girl,' she told him as she strained to hear above the crackles of the uncertain long distance connection. 'I've got a sink full of dirty socks'. Said Dad.

We had often joined him in the U.S. and on trips back home the maisonette had filled up with weird anomalies like long-haired goatskin carpets. These were ideal for concealing the mummified remains of the dead mice that Grandpa had failed to notice when he'd come in to feed the cat (and subsequently trodden on, so that when eventually discovered they were flat as well).

I was seven years old at the time we moved to Harrow and I quickly became friendly with an older girl called Poppy who lived around the corner from our new home, in a very angular and modern house that had a flat roof. The bedrooms were downstairs and the kitchen and living area were upstairs. I imagine that nowadays it would be listed as a wonder of Post-Modernist architecture, but unfortunately it was demolished to make way for an access road to a new housing estate that developers went on to build in the fields behind Sudbury Court Drive. However, at the time the best thing about that 'upside down' house was that it had a pool; and it was whilst swimming there happily one summers day, that I first espied the impish little face of an envious next-door neighbour peering over the fence.

That face belonged to Janet, who in actual fact lived next door but one, but she was in playing with her own next door neighbour, a girl named Nicky. These were children of privilege who lived in large detached houses with enormous back-gardens and they were very different when compared to scruffy me who had suddenly come up in the world very fast. I had been used to playing in the rough back alleys of 'maisonette-land' in Neasden. In those early days, from the age of around three or four, gangs of us children would climb over the concrete, bindweed covered fence that bordered our alley and trespass in the grounds of an imposing factory known as 'The Press' (where angry folks would bang on the windows and tell us to, 'Clear off'). Then we disappeared under yet another fence, to run wild in the fields spotted with yellow gorse that surrounded The Welsh Harp reservoir (where Cream also larked about in their first promotional music film). Along our alleys the coal men would come with their heavy sacks slung across their backs to fill the bunkers that sat in our tiny gardens and sometimes Dad would haul me over his shoulders and shout, 'Sack of coal, sack of coal', to my great delight.

But now I had to adjust to the life of the better off and make new friends amongst them and that wasn't always easy. They thought I was a spoilt brat and Janet and I were sworn enemies for ages as we fought over the asthmatic charms of Nicky. But inexplicably one day, we suddenly clicked with each other and from then on poor Nicky never got a look in. Janet was two years older than I and although her other siblings were privately educated, she went to school at what was then known as 'Blackwell Secondary Modern', later to become the infamous 'Hatch End High'.

We began our relationship by playing cowboys ('I've lost me caps!') around the streets, or we entertained ourselves upstairs in my room with the Barbies. We had many trips down Sudbury Court Drive to Prangleys sweet shop that later turned into Forbuoys. We made up our own language and we laughed so much that we were very often to be found lying prostrate and crying upon the pavement. We invented a whole new vocabulary that spread out amongst our friends and soon everyone knew that 'Doris' meant somebody old, boring and straight-laced and there were other equally ridiculous and incomprehensible things that we and a very few others found to be deeply hilarious. (Such as singing the refrain *'Raspberry Rimplop'* along to the *'Hare Krishna'* tune; particularly when encountering those bald, orange clad devotees jingling their bells and dancing along past Kensington Market, where we had gone to buy our 'Love Beads'.)

One of our very early adventures involved us collaring two boys who lived on Sudbury Court Drive and we went off into the Hill fields with them. I liked the blond one called Michael and Janet fancied the darker one, named John. Unfortunately, it all went disastrously wrong when we somehow inadvertently paired up with each other's choice and I ended up in my Mum and Dad's bedroom with this very young John character. It was my very first French kiss, but I was reasonably confident about it, having been previously instructed on the mechanics of this type of kissing by Poppy. He was quite surprised that I seemed to know what I was doing and he came and knocked on the door for me the next day. By this time though, I definitely thought, 'no thanks' and got rid of him by telling him that I was in fact only ten, when I had originally put my age as thirteen.

Janet and I gradually progressed to spending our Saturdays catching the 182 bus into Harrow where we purchased Biba nail varnish, went to The Wimpy Bar and then smoked Consulate cigarettes as we walked home over the Hill deciding which houses we were going to live in when we grew up. Janet later got a Saturday job in the Chelsea Girl boutique there and then I would go in and see her and swoon over a bottle green velvet skirt that I eventually managed to acquire. We went to Blackwell Secondary Modern school discos and parties in the leafy streets of Pinner and Hatch End, which I'm glad to report, involved a lot of snogging. Parties were often held in garages and would begin with the long-haired and Tank Top clad boys swigging cider at one end and us giggly girls sipping Cinzano in our maxi skirts at the other. But after enough Slade singles had gone under the stylus the two groups got together.

In March '73, Janet and I went to see Slade at Wembley Arena and it was a great gig, with Jim Lea jumping about like a madman in a red glitter suit and the whole place literally shook to the rhythmic stomping of thousands of pairs of platform boots. Slade are still a very underrated band. Then Janet got into heavier music; she had all the Led Zeppelin albums and she wore a long red velvet dress and an Afghan coat. A mark of coolness was apparently how many tracks you could sit in the Lotus position for before your legs dropped off! She also introduced me to Neil Young's 'After the Gold Rush' and 'Harvest' LPs, but when I played them at home my Dad said that poor Neil sounded, 'Pathetic and weedy.'

On the day of the Baker Gurvitz Army Rainbow gig, Janet and I got tarted up in our dark blue satin bomber jackets, flared jeans and platform shoes. A limo duly arrived to ferry us there and we both took great pleasure in waving to all the snooty neighbours out of the car window. Once at the gig, we stood with Mum at the entrance to the dressing room tunnel and were denied access by a zealous bouncer. We said, 'Look mate, we know the guy in charge, his name is Jack, just get him and he'll confirm who we are, etc, etc.'

But no, this bouncer thought we were a bunch of liars and said as much very rudely. This of course, resulted in him getting a thick ear from Mother, who bashed him so hard that her heavy jade bracelet broke into a thousand pieces and scattered noisily across the stone floor of the corridor. Then, as if by magic, 'Jack' suddenly did appear to let us in. We told Dad about our difficulties, so he had a fit and went and smashed the naughty bouncer's room up. I felt a bit sorry for the guy I have to say, but power trips can often end badly. We had to walk across the back of the stage to get to our seats. This resulted in much whistling and cat calling from the audience. How we loved it!

That exciting walk across the stage pretending we were famous, reminded me of the time when I had been with my parents at the 1967 Windsor Jazz Festival and Cream, Jeff Beck and Rod Stewart were on the bill. Rod had elected to look after me for my Mum and Dad for about half an hour or so. He kept me entertained by clowning about and really making me laugh. Never being one to remain unmoved by a pretty face, whatever my age, I quickly became well smitten. Somebody or other then suggested that I might like to introduce a song. Rod led me to the front of the stage and reminded me to, 'Mind the wires love', as I stood for a moment, completely mesmerised by the reflected light that bounced back at me from the many spectacle wearing members of the audience.

'This is Ginger Baker's daughter Nettie' said Rod, 'and she's going to introduce the next song'.

He handed me the mic. Rather tentatively I introduced 'Hi Ho Silver Lining' and everybody clapped.

When we were finally settled into our seats that night at The Rainbow in 1975, I decided that I needed the loo, so Jap and I trailed off on a long trek to find one. On the way back, we got completely lost and somehow ended up back outside the theatre, frantically banging on the fire escape doors until someone took pity on us and let us back in.

Out of breath and laughing, we sat back down again, the band played one number, the drummer stopped and said, 'Sorry folks, but I just need to go for a piss!'

Janet looked at me, 'Now I know where you get it from' she said.

After the gig, we all trawled back stage again to have champagne and fraternize with the natives. Dad was shaking the bottle wildly like a Grand Prix racing driver on the podium, so it fizzed everywhere and I hid behind a sofa with Janet's (not my own you notice) coat over my head. Then we went off to find the private party that was being held in the circle bar. I helped to carry a very unsteady Dad along a corridor in the theatre. He was saying, 'It's a good job I'm not drunk' (which always meant he was), and we bumped straight in to Lee.

Lee was a roadie who was then aged about twenty-four. He was extremely pleasant to look at, with high cheekbones, a pointed face, long, straight black hair and he was a right Jack the Lad. I had first clapped eyes on him at a boring recording session I had been to with Dad and after I had enlivened the interminable hours in the studio by staring at him, I renamed him 'Ace Face' to myself and made up a song about him on the drive home (no, I'm not telling you how it goes).

He used to play football with Dad sometimes on Sundays up at Robert Stigwood's huge, half-timbered, Jacobean house in Brooks Hill, Stanmore. This mansion, known as 'The Old Barn', was (and still is) a magnificent example of late Tudor architecture, boasting an incredible oak staircase complete with grinning gargoyles and an impossibly high ceiling hall from which hung dark pennants of heavy and ancient cobwebs. Even the spiders wore ruffs and played lutes. The football up at Stigwood's became quite a regular thing for a while and one day a familiar looking bloke in a flat cap knocked at our front door and asked me for directions. It turned out to be the pianist and singer Alan Price. Anyway, it was the highlight of my week if Dad brought Lee home afterwards for tea.

The previous August Dad had hosted a birthday party up in town. Lee and Adrian (Gurvitz) had asked if they could take the thirteen year-old me in Adrian's two-seater black Corvette Stingray. I was nodding, 'Yes, yes!' And oh dear, I had to sit on Lee's lap all the way. We dodged through the traffic and accelerated through the brightly lit London streets, whilst surprising things happened to my undergarments. At the time I found it to be an interesting and not unpleasant experience, but nowadays you might call it molestation.

'You can't just walk past her!' Dad shouted to Lee in the echoing corridor of The Rainbow, 'Give my daughter a kiss!'

I nearly fell through the floor with embarrassment, as Lee obliged. When we had finally got Dad to the party at The Rainbow bar, I noticed that Adrian's face was covered with silver glitter; and as Janet was plastered in the stuff, this appeared to me to be an obvious give away. But luckily for Janet, his American girlfriend (who was known to us privately as 'Gee They Got a Band', in reference to a character in a TV commercial for beefburgers starring Sandra Dickinson) didn't seem to realise. After Janet had been pursued around the bar several times by a strange man called Alphonso, we adjourned to The Kensington Hilton for a meal. Once at the table, Adrian's girlfriend looked up from the menu and uttered the immortal words, 'Ginger, what's a prawn?'

The evening's entertainment culminated in a now legendary journey home in the silver Jensen FF, when the man who was too drunk to stand insisted on driving us all home. Everyone acquiesced, though to be fair to Mum she did voice some concerns as to whether it really was a great idea. We reached a top speed of 145 MPH down the West Way (A 40), a fact that Dad proudly informed us of, adding as a rider to Janet, 'Don't tell your father you've been this fast.'

Now Janet's dad (a very nice man named Douglas) was a Quantity Surveyor. A profession which we always associated with the comedian Marty Feldman's (Monty Python: Bookshop) sketch 'Ethel the Aardvark goes Quantity Surveying.' Douglas was also a Lay Preacher and I don't think he'd have been too thrilled to learn of his daughter's fate at the hands of a maniac rock star, but I very much doubt that she ever told him.

Anyway, as you might imagine, we reached Harrow quite quickly and the *coup de grace* came about when Dad reversed the Jensen into the front of his new Range Rover as he parked (if you can call it that) outside our house. As an encore, he stood in the hall for a while, banging his head against the wall and moaning about it. Finally, a very drunk Nettie walked a very drunk Janet back up the road to her house and that was in my opinion, the perfect end to a perfect evening.

Not long afterwards, I was at The Speakeasy club in town with Mum and Dad where I was thrilled to see the two sax players from The Glitterband, dressed identically in their silver suits, walk past me in the foyer. But then the Baker Gurvitz Army marched off to the States to do some more arguing and the fun was over. On May 1st I wrote 'Tomorrow I'm going to Sheryl's for the weekend.' I was just a day away from meeting Johnny Gale.

CHAPTER THREE
Chingford Hatch: 1975

'..and I think it's going to be a long long time.'
(Rocket Man: Elton John.)

I first went to Stella's school in early 1971, after I'd got expelled from Heathfield's School for Girls in Harrow. What a very uptight place that was. They chucked me out because my Dad had been featured in the News of the World under the lurid banner headline of, 'Pop Stars Who Take Drugs!' alongside The Rolling Stones. As a result of this, I wasn't deemed suitable for their establishment, though they made some other excuses about naughty behaviour and by the way, thigh high, black, wet look boots were not on the uniform list either, who would've thought it?

Soon a letter arrived with a request that I leave the school at the beginning of the Spring Term, 1971. It *was* a mildly embarrassing day for me when in reaction to this correspondence Dad stormed up the school with his hair in a ponytail and sat moodily on the stairs as a sea of children flowed nervously around him. Once in the Headmistress's office, he loudly accused her of being, 'A frustrated old lesbian', before carting me off, as curious six-formers hung out of the first floor windows. After this, it was decided that a stage school would be best for me, so that's how I met Sheryl.

When I first walked into the classroom in that February

1971, I was barely ten years old and she had just celebrated her twelfth birthday. I guess it was because of lack of space and teaching staff that we were all lumped together in rough age ranges and put in for our exams at different times. Sheryl was an enigmatic, dark-eyed Romany looking girl and we hit it off straight away. It didn't take long for her to become known as 'Peril' and for me to answer to 'Bakewell Jam Tart'. Sheryl was good at Maths and I was good at English, so a mutually beneficial relationship was quickly established, which involved the passing of notes backwards and forwards under the desks. She also taught me the important schoolgirl corruptions of the English language, 'Haigy Paigy' and 'Uvaguv', so that we could talk secretly without being understood by adults or the uninitiated.

Sheryl's parents Rita and Bob ran Truman's Sports Ground in The Avenue, Higham's Park. This was a suburb of Greater London that had once been part of Essex and whose streets ran alongside great swathes of common land on the edge of Epping Forest. Truman's Sport's Ground consisted of a large football field and a pavilion with a hall, bar and kitchen downstairs and living quarters upstairs. The decent sized hall was the ideal place for sporting functions and parties as well as other community based activities and at weekends Sheryl used it to teach ballet to little kids. In the early years we would put our pointed shoes on and dress ourselves up in voluminous dance skirts of blue and green sequinned chiffon. Then we would cavort around in the hall and out on the sunny, empty sport's field like two demented latter day Isadora Duncans. Over the next four years, I spent so many weekends there that her Mum referred to it as my 'second home.'

In the spring of 1975, Sheryl had discovered that the

tasty young footballers she met there on Sundays normally drank in a pub at the bottom of Chingford Hatch called The Horseless Carriage and that weekend she asked me to go there with her. On Saturday 3rd May, we carefully got ourselves plastered in slap and self-consciously arranged our long and newly washed, centre parted hair before we set off for the pub. The two of us then meandered slowly along the suburban streets and cut through narrow alleys over hung with white May blossom. With trepidation in our hearts, we reached the tree lined Hatch and there the striking white Modernist parade of shops dominated the landscape looking for all the world as though The Queen Mary had weighed anchor in the great green sea of Epping Forest. The Horseless Carriage public house was just a tug in comparison, moored alongside.

As its name suggests, 'The Horseless' as we later so fondly referred to it, consisted of a semi-circular building flanked by an old railway carriage that served as a restaurant. We walked boldly into the spacious bar and I was soon drinking Bacardi and orange as Sheryl introduced me to the lads she knew. Within about ten minutes I found myself very taken with the one that they called Johnny Gale and I thought he looked like a darker version of that dishy Marty bloke from the band The New Seekers. Johnny Gale wasn't all that tall and he was incredibly slight. But he had good shoulders, very long, chestnut hair and dark eyes. He was a flirty joker of a lad, who proceeded to show off and fool about in order to impress us teens and he certainly made a good job of it. I learned during the odd sensible bit in the banter that he was a drummer (can you believe it?) and without a flicker of conscience he said that he was nineteen when I asked him. At the same time, I may have claimed to be fifteen.

Then he mentioned that his band was playing at a pub named 'The Tower' the very next night. Poor Sheryl had to suffer me swooning and sighing over this vision all the way home and after I had pestered her non-stop for several hours, she agreed that we could go and see Johnny Gale in action.

So the very next evening, we got into her Dad's blue Ford Consul Estate and he gave us a lift to 'The Tower Flanagans' in Walthamstow. The pub loomed up in the light evening, its brickwork supporting a rickety structure that proclaimed 'Tower' in letters of lurid orange neon. We excitedly clomped inside, all eyeliner and zip-up cardigans, having no qualms about being well under age and we easily got served with our Bacardi and Cokes. Then I got out my packet of ten Consulates and lit up in what I hoped was a sophisticated manner. The band appeared on the little stage at the far end of the bar, sorting out their equipment. John was tottering around his drum kit in white platform shoes. He was also wearing a fitted, dark coloured, long sleeved T-shirt and skin-tight, midnight blue velvet trousers that rather disconcertingly left nothing at all to the imagination. Around his neck was knotted a flimsy black chiffon scarf. I took a swig of my Bacardi for support and whispered to Sheryl, 'Oh my God, he's wearing make-up!' And so he was.

His dark kohl rimmed eyes and long hair gave him a disturbingly androgynous effect. I use the word 'disturbing' 'cos after all I was only fourteen and apart from seeing Sweet on Top of the Pops, you didn't come across a lot of men wearing make-up in suburbia in those days. I know we had Bowie, Bolan, Ferry and Roy Wood who was just plain barmy, but my contemporaries and I always laughed nervously at them. We weren't quite sure how to take things like the outrageous get up of Sweet's bass player Steve Priest and Rob Davis from Mud who wore Christmas decorations in his ears; because we had trouble understanding what was going on. Here in the Tower Flanagans, it dawned on me for the first (but not the last) time, that there was something very sexy indeed about men in make-up. John soon spotted us and he came over to say, 'Hello'. He was clutching a pint of lager and I noticed that he bit his nails. I was nearly knocked out by a blast of his 'West' aftershave and then he went to play his set.

'Can I have your autograph?' I asked breathlessly when he came off stage. Johnny Gale took the pen that I proffered and wrote the word 'God' with a flourish in the back of my diary, as though it was something particularly amusing. Maybe it was a pun on the old 'Clapton is God' graffiti? Though if so it was lost on me. Then amazingly, he asked me for my phone number and when I gave it to him he said that he would ring me during the week. Love couldn't be this easy could it? It was far too much to believe that an attractive and unattainable older guy like this would be interested in a gawky, skinny, flat-chested and very young girl like me. I sat by the phone every evening that week and he never did call.

But he did play at The Tower again the following Sunday and once more I hectored poor Sheryl into going along with me. This time I had put some photographs of Dad in my bag, because John had said that he really didn't believe that I was Ginger Baker's daughter. Well, why on earth would a fourteen-year-old girl make him up as a parent in 1975 is all that I can say; Ringo Starr perhaps or Cozy Powell maybe?

However, I got over that hurdle and my friends and I were so impressed by our own local Glamrock star that in a very short time, several of us young ladies were tarting about with our own black chiffon *'John scarves'* tied gracefully around our necks.

It soon became a regular thing for us to walk down to The Horseless Carriage from Sheryl's on summer evenings, dressed in our favourite high waisted skirts or wide legged button fly trousers and the inevitable platform shoes. The young lads that we met there were obviously older than us and certainly old enough to drink legally. There was Roy 'the chef', who with his spiky dark blond mullet was cheeky and full of life, there was Dell, a stocky blond, Nicky, a beanpole, with short dark hair and there was also Arthur, who had long fair tresses and a 'tache and often made us laugh with his 'Trimphone' impressions. For some reason we always referred to Arthur as 'Alfred of The Burnt Cakes' (but why?).

There were many other long or short-haired Micks, Mickys, Johnnys and whoever and even a 'Baldy', which speaks for itself. Anita joined us one night and she decided that she rather liked Dell. Then Sheryl became fond of a guy called Steve. He was a striking blond, with brown eyes and a stunning white smile. One morning at school, Sheryl informed us that she'd seen Steve at Walthamstow Central the previous evening with another girl. But in a spirit of optimism we decided that it must have been his sister!

Whilst Sheryl, Anita and I, were haunting The Horseless Carriage on a regular basis, John and the other boys also hung around the Sport's Ground a bit with us, where we would help out behind the bar after the football at the weekends. Instead of pouring the drinks that we got bought for us we'd save the money so that we could have enough to go out with in the evenings. The atmosphere was friendly and the happy little place smelt reassuringly of beer and fags. I enjoyed trading banter whilst pulling pints and I was always having the piss taken out of my posh accent because I pronounced all the T's in Light & Bitter.

On those nights that we went down The Horseless, we'd walk back to Sheryl's and sit outside the pavilion talking whilst using the downstairs kitchen to make coffee and toast, before waving the lads off and going upstairs. This upper story had a long, blue-carpeted corridor, which gave off a not unpleasant odour of cabbages, boiled milk and Trixie the dog (another dog, Tara, a German Shepherd, lived in a kennel outside). There was a tiny kitchen upstairs as well and that joined the cosy living room where we hung out and played Pontoon for pennies whilst listening to 'Elton John's Greatest Hits' (1974) and The Beatles' 'Sergeant Peppers' LP's.

We sang along to 'Rocket Man', 'Crocodile Rock' and 'Border Song' (*'I have seen the spectre, he has been here too'*). We got into Elton's new 'Captain Fantastic' album that was just out, with its great tracks; 'We all Fall in Love Sometimes', 'Tower of Babel' (*'hungry hunters tracking down the hours'*), 'Someone Saved my Life Tonight', and 'Better off Dead.'

'There was a face on the hoardings
that someone had drawn on
And just enough time for the night
to pass by without warning
Away in the distance there's a blue flashing light
Someone's in trouble somewhere tonight.
As the flickering neon stands ready to fuse
The wind blows away all of yesterdays news.'
(Elton John: Better Off Dead)

One day, as Elton sang and I gazed out over the shed roofs and the lines of washing that had been left to dry in the adjoining back gardens, I dedicated 'Your Song' to Johnny Gale (and 'excuse me,' I had not 'forgotten' that his eyes were brown).

Then one Sunday I bumped into him again at Sheryl's whilst I was collecting glasses. He hung about looking friendly but I made a point of ignoring him and so the next time I had to walk past him he stopped me.

'Don't say hello then'

'Hello' I answered and gave him a dirty look (we regularly practised these).

'What's that for?'

'Just because.'

'You're playing hard to get aren't you?'

'No, you are.'

We soon fell into conversation, he said that he still had my number and might give me a ring (but we both knew he wouldn't).

Luckily for them, the footballing lads of Chingford were spared for a week at the end of May when Sheryl and her family took me to The Isle of Wight with them and we stayed at the Ladbroke's Holiday Camp at Nodes Point. By this time I had as a Rock Star's progeny, been all over the world so you may think that this one would have been a bit of a come down in my eyes.

Our first family holiday as rich folks had been to Mexico City and Acapulco in 1967, where Dad had delighted in cutting crabs in half with a large machete, until my mother stopped him. *'Down in Acapulco'* as whatshisface sings, I got very badly sunburnt on the beach one day when Mum and Dad got so out of it smoking Acapulco Gold with the locals, that by their own admission they totally forgot that they even had a child at all. We flew back to Mexico City in a light aircraft held together with elastic bands and Dad pointed out the volcano Popocatépetl, whose icy surface glinted diamond-like above the clouds.

After that when my siblings (Leda, then brother Kofi in 1969) had come into the world, we went to the exotic Caribbean island of Jamaica on two separate occasions. We flew there first class on BOAC and stayed at the luxurious resorts of Tryal and Frenchman's Cove and we even met Errol Flynn's widow Patrice Wymore. Dad was so taken with Jamaica that he had his silver Jensen flown out especially. So we cruised through the fields of moonlit sugar cane that whispered close to the ruins of the old plantation houses as The Band's 'Music from the Big Pink' came blaring out of the Four Track.

'I see my light come shining, from the west down to the east / any day now, any day now, I shall be released...'

We visited the shell of the notorious Rose Hall and we were even welcomed into a sinister 'Maroon' village up in the hills, where allegedly no other whites had ever set foot. Ooeer.

Mr Baker said some fairly amusing things on our holidays. In Morocco circa 1970 a market trader in Marrakesh touched my blonde hair longingly and offered my parents 600 camels for my hand.

'I don't think they would all fit in my garden' came Dad's reply.

In a luxurious Carribean restaurant around the same year, our family meal was constantly being interrupted by the very loud exclamations of some rich Americans at a nearby table. Mr B was getting increasingly wound up, whilst Mrs B was trying to calm him down, but inevitably he could stand it no longer and stood up to bellow, 'Do you mind, there are people trying to sleep here!' at the top of his voice, as several waiters ran away laughing.

On a 1971 trip to Bude in Cornwall we sat waiting for our dinner in the plush hotel dining room when a young waiter sidled over.

'My friend doesn't believe you're Ginger Baker' said the boy.

We all looked at each other in silence for a moment, because of course we knew that an outburst was about to take place.

'I couldn't give a monkey's left tit what your friend thinks,' shouted Dad, 'now just get me my bloody food.'

Yet I suppose the crowning moment of all these had to be on our early Mexico trip, when we endured the thirteen-hour flight aboard a Qantas jet. Dad was leaning over the little table drawing and his long red hair obscured his craggy bearded face. A camp steward approached his seat pushing a trolley.

'Cigarettes Madam?' He intoned innocently and got no reaction. Undaunted he decided to give it another go.

'Cigarettes Madam?' He repeated.

The look on his face was an absolute picture as he suddenly beheld Dad's hairy, scowling visage.

'What?'

'Terribly sorry Sir.'

Cue vast amusement for the whole of that aisle (except Dad of course).

Yes I had been to places that nearly every child I knew could only dream about. Such as The Hawaiian Hilton on Oahu, where from the balcony you could see the famous Diamond Head Volcano ('book 'em Danno') and round the corner from Waikiki Beach at Pearl Harbour a helpful soul brought to our attention the numbers of body bags (filled with heroin, so rumour had it) that were coming in from Vietnam.

With Cream and Blind Faith of course we'd toured all over the U.S.A. and in the August of '74, we went to Marbella *en famile* along with Paul Gurvitz and his wife; where we ate in exclusive restaurants and went horse riding (galloping) through deserted villages inhabited only by stray dogs, in the hot and silent hills (which I hated). But The Isle of Wight with Sheryl and her folks in that May of 1975 was the best holiday that I have ever had.

I wore cheesecloth smocks and white jeans rolled up to the knee with long red, white and blue striped socks and huge platform shoes. We were plastered in tons of make-up and took the piss out of Bay City Roller's fans. At that time I thought they were rubbish, but in hindsight I think they are marvellous. This was the time when Les of The Rollers got done for knocking someone over in his car, so we changed the lyrics of The Beatle's 'A Day in the Life' to,

'I heard the news today oh boy, a Bay City Roller ran over an old lady.' Sorry Les!

There was a ballroom at this camp where we played bingo (which I loved) and every night we'd go down there to see and hear the resident band who were called The T-Set. They were fairly young and Sheryl and I would sit right up the front and write requests on beer mats like 'play Quo' and 'no Doris music', which we held up to them, so we got quite friendly.

They took us out one night, and we all squashed into a Mini and went to a nightclub named Babalu's. Sheryl hooked up with the drummer this time for a change, whilst Wayne, who was the ginger-haired guitarist, escorted me. He also gave me his autograph and mercifully he didn't try to be clever and write something witty like someone else we know. On the last night we had another date, but this time only with two "Scottish gits" who wore enormous flares, platform shoes, woolly tank tops, had silly hair and sported unpleasant little 'bum fluff' moustaches.

By the night of 1st June, hooray, we were back in The Horseless. We met up with some other locally based mates of Sheryl's and happily crowded up to the bar, shouting and jostling elbows, whilst Sheryl, who was the oldest, bought the drinks. Knots of people stood about outside; laughter carried over the sounds of the cars accelerating up Chingford Hatch and the birds still singing joyfully in the summer dusk. I shouted to Sheryl that I was off on one of my usual nine hundred trips to the loo, but I never got there because as I pushed my way through the crowd I collided head on with Johnny Gale.

We seemed to hit it off right away and it was one of those rare occasions in life when everything seems to go right. Yes, here was Steve, very interested in Sheryl and now here was John, doing quite a decent impression of being interested in me. The other girls who had been hanging out with us went home and as Sheryl and I waited around expectantly Steve and John elected to walk us both back to Truman's. We went along The Bramblings two by two, talking all the while. Through to Abbott's Crescent and into The Avenue, then we made the right turn into the alleyway that led down to The Sport's Ground. Once there, the four of us mucked about and had a laugh making bacon sandwiches and coffee in the kitchen, whilst John decided to make a big show of pretending to be scared of Sheryl's dogs. At least I hope he was pretending.

After a while, John and I went to sit on one of the benches outside the pavilion. The pale roses were nodding ghostly and luminous in the darkness. Night breezes blew across the deserted sports field and lights glowed in the windows of the houses opposite. Somebody drew their curtains and somewhere a dog barked, as Johnny Gale and I smoked cigarettes and talked softly about little things in a big wide world. Then he decided that he ought to be leaving, so I walked with him slowly back down the driveway and he mentioned that I seemed like a bit of an 'idealist' to him. Yes, my ideal being that you'd bloody fancy me! I didn't consider the fact that I was too young or think about any age gap at all. By now we were standing at the very end of the alleyway and I could see Falmouth Avenue branching off on the opposite side of the road. A tall wooden fence kept us close and undiscovered in its shadow. He had the grace to put his arms round me and say nice things and kiss me in perhaps a not that over enthusiastic fashion. His lips lightly brushed my face and he was sweet and gentle compared to anything I had so far experienced at the hands of callow youths. I could quite happily have dragged that moment out for hours, but sensing this, Mr Gale was swift to act. 'See you when I see you' he said and he walked away.

His lean frame was silhouetted in the gloom, his hair flopped upon his shoulders and his shadow stretched long upon the pavement, as I stood motionless and watched him disappear up The Avenue towards The Hatch. Oh dear. My heart sank about a thousand foot when I realised that he didn't really like me that much at all. I turned reluctantly and stumbled sadly back along the stony, uneven path and I could still smell his aftershave wafting up from my T-shirt. Then I came upon Sheryl saying goodbye to Steve in the shadows and when he had gone, we drifted in whispering and giggling so much that her parents told us off for being late.

The following Monday at school Sheryl handed me a note decorated with arrow pierced hearts filled with the initials, 'S 4 S' and 'G 4 J', in which she had written amongst other things, that I was 'Soon to be Mrs J. Gale (you hope).' With a young girl's optimism, I clung to the belief that he just might possibly change his mind and I was forever dragging Sheryl and her hapless mates in and out of the various pubs in the vicinity in the forlorn hope of bumping in to him accidentally on purpose; as you do. In fact, I went to Chingford more than ever before, mainly in the hope of meeting John again even if long distance swooning was all that I could hope for.

On the last Saturday in June, Sheryl had a party and Anita's Dad gave us a lift all the way to Higham's Park in his dark blue Citroen DS. The journey itself was a bit of haul *'from the west down to the east'* so to speak; in those days before the road building maniacs had decided to construct all the new bypasses on the North Circular. The sun was low in the sky as we passed myriads of tired Saturday shoppers making their weary way homewards and Ni and I looked forward eagerly to the coming night's events. Finally we arrived at our destination and it was, 'Yes, bye and thanks Anita's Dad' without a backwards glance as the poor man had to contemplate negotiating his way back again along that awful road.

Sheryl met us at the back door and I handed her my offering of a bottle of Bacardi, before barging upstairs where we laughed and gossiped happily as we put the finishing touches to our outfits. I was wearing a floaty, calf length, blue halter neck dress, cork soled platform sandals and 'Dioressence' perfume. We went down to wait for the first party goers to arrive. We gulped our drinks nervously, anticipating a bit of action, as the first bars of Sweet's 1973 hit 'Blockbuster' reverberated through the rafters. As the revelry got under way I was accosted by a couple of Essex girls outside the ladies toilets. The louder of the two grabbed my arm and shouted drunkenly, 'Your

Dad's Ginger Rogers!'

Then the Horseless crew (now known as 'The Drunkards') turned up. Unfortunately, Steve had brought a girl with him (a terrible crime), but undeterred by such perfidy, Sheryl went off to dance with someone else. Johnny Gale breezed in without a girl thank God, so once more we got together and we spent most of the night slow dancing and talking non stop and once or twice even kissing again so perhaps my luck *had* changed? As the night wore on, we ended up sitting together in the darkened upstairs sitting room, where the music was low and people were murmuring and laughing softly, whilst above our heads the net curtains blew in noiselessly at the window. John asked me if I would go for a walk with him, but something about the look in his eyes when he said this, prompted me to refuse. *'Let's go for a little walk, under the moon of love...'* (Under The Moon Of Love: Showaddywaddy)

So he said that he must be going and he disappeared at around three in the morning. That took all the joy out of the previous hours that we had spent together and I could have kicked myself.

Inevitably, the dawn broke and we discovered that some tosser had stolen all the fags out of the bar. However, we managed to smooth it all over and after doing the obligatory tidying up, I headed off back to the west. I sat on a Met line tube and my glittery party make-up was still smudged across my face. I gazed sadly out over the tangled, bramble strewn embankments as the carriages rumbled rhythmically over the tracks. In my head I replayed the confusing sequence of recent events that had starred Mr Gale. Was anything ever going to happen with us or not?

'Wise men say it looks like rain today
It crackled on the speakers and
trickled down the sleepy subway trains,
The heavy eyes could hardly hold us
Aching legs that often told us
It's all worth it
We all fall in love sometimes'
(Elton John: 'We All Fall in Love Sometimes')

Later that day, Sheryl rang and told me that John had approached her tentatively at the bar after football and said, 'I bet your friend is cross with me' and that he thought it was all his fault.

A few nights later he was spotted in The Horseless with a girl and then I found out that he was in fact twenty-three and *not* nineteen as he had hitherto maintained.

In July, we did the school show and then I caught Chicken Pox from my sister and brother. This meant that I was 'Spotty Muldoon' and off the scene for a while and I couldn't get down to The Horseless. Sheryl and Anita continued to report back to me whenever they saw John and they even bought me a 'Get Well' card, which they got all the lads (including Johnny Gale) to sign.

I finally managed to get back down there on the 26th July, when I spent a week at Sheryl's. I saw John again that very night; all was instantly forgiven of course in the light of his scintillating company and we talked the hours away as usual. But our in-depth conversations are now forever lost in time and our words have drifted off unremembered into the ether, which is a waste really, even if it was a load of drivel. Of course I got my hopes up yet again, but on Wednesday 30th July something happened that changed all that for a while.

That night, John had been strangely absent from the

pub. Dell and Nick had offered to walk Sheryl and Anita home, so I was trailing slowly and sadly along behind like a gooseberry. As we came around the corner into The Bramblings, we practically walked into a young couple kissing under the lamppost in our path. The darkness receded to reveal them entwined, close and oblivious of all else, bathed romantically in the soft glow of the light. The others forged on ahead unconcernedly, but the couple loomed unnaturally large in my sight as the unpleasant realisation hit me that the male of the two was indeed none other than Johnny Gale. I pushed past my startled friends, babbling incoherently with tears streaming down my face and they thought, 'Oh there goes Miss Drama again, getting all worked up over nothing.' Concerned residents of The Avenue peered out through their net curtains. Tut, tut, the youth of today.

Back at Sheryl's and out of that cruel night, I retreated into the relative safety of the upstairs sitting room. I raced to the record player, manoeuvred the needle over the track 'Don't Let The Sun Go Down On Me' and turned it up. Then I sat and felt very sorry for myself as we drank our weak coffee out of brown glass mugs and watched the undissolved granules floating in circles on the top.

'*I can't light no more of your darkness,*' sang Elton mournfully in the little room at Higham's Park. The poignancy of loss eh?

Now I had already planned to have a party at my place the following weekend and 'The Drunkards' had of course been invited. But on the night in question John was conspicuous by his absence, so it would seem that he *had* been aware of my presence in The Bramblings that night and maybe he heard me running off or perhaps the other lads had told him? Whatever the case, my much anticipated revels were now reduced to nothing without him. Ahhh. Johnny Gale and I became estranged; he didn't speak to me because I suppose he felt guilty and also he was with his girlfriend now whenever we went to the pub.

Sheryl and Anita continued to go about with various lads and one night a guy we knew walked me back from the Horseless, but who should we bump into along the way but Johnny Gale and his beloved. 'Hello', we intoned awkwardly and went on walking, but I looked back regretfully. Without the hope of him in my life Chingford had lost its glamour. The heady days of the Horseless, football Sundays and mad times at Larkswood swimming pool were drawing to a close.   My Dad had started to play Polo at a place near Richmond Park and I began to attend various events over there, taking Sheryl, Anita and Louise along with me. The Sport's Ground began to look desolate as the winds of autumn swept across it, tearing the petals from the yellow roses and sending them spiralling aimlessly around the pavilion.

'Now the wind has changed direction and I have to leave.' (Elton John: 'Border Song')

CHAPTER FOUR
Flambards: 1976

In 1975, I had emerged albeit cautiously, as a person in my own right; following a limited amount of my own interests and experiencing something of life in the way that so called 'normal' people went about it. Unfortunately, my failure to secure the affections of Johnny Gale, had led me to experience a feeling of disenchantment with all things ordinary, because surely I was destined for better?

I can't say that I ever took much notice of the traditional '70's socio-political overview of poverty and strife. The power cuts of 1973 had been fun and were merely an excuse to have a bath by candlelight. At home we became anxious that the water in the tropical fish tank would get cold and as a result Mum and Dad could be found frantically boiling water on the gas hob and then pouring it into the tank to keep the temperature up (poached Angel Fish anyone?) As well as this, the contents of the Deep Freeze tended to melt and then Mum would run about the kitchen in her red fox fur coat (heating gone off) holding up soggy bits of meat and swearing.

One dark winter's afternoon, Mum drove us out of Harrods car park in her pale yellow Mini Cooper S (Radford conversion) and as we pulled out into the street, the lights along a whole block suddenly went out. It was dramatic and exciting when it seemed that civilisation was teetering on the edge of the blackout. Strikes were okay. It was only the mention of nuclear ones that worried me. Ted Heath and Harold Wilson, how much notice did I take of these things apart from Mike Yarwood doing impressions of them on TV? My Dad moaned a lot about having to pay income tax of 98p in the pound and Grandma complained that, 'The unions are holding this country to ransom', in the manner of Thora Hird playing an unsympathetic character in a nineteen-sixties 'Kitchen Sink' drama.

By 1976 the rantings of the early Punks began to surface as the voice of a disaffected and disillusioned youth, uncertain of what their future held. 'No Future' indeed and I was the perfect age to get involved in all of this, but my circumstances were totally different. The only slightly punk related thing I did do was to buy my first pair of straight jeans and some non-platform ankle boots with a zip up the front. I wore them on Twelfth Night, when Mum, Dad and I piled into one of the two Jensen FF's that we owned and drove down to Eric Clapton's house in Surrey.

Our fat low profile tyres crunched up the gravel drive that curved elegantly in front of his beautiful Italianate mansion, Hurtwood Edge. The house was set like a red jewel in its own dark green labyrinth of a garden, whilst giant and majestic Redwood trees stood guard over it. The powerful Chrysler V8 engine gave a throaty growl as Dad revved up outside the front door to announce our arrival and then cut the ignition. Eric and Pattie appeared at the door together and ushered us inside where we were greeted by their other guests who just happened to be George Harrison and his girlfriend.

Well, this was a bit of a step up from serving Light & Bitter in Highams Park wasn't it?

'Hey, look at me guys' I thought and I began to hum, '*If My Friends Could See Me Now*' like Shirley Maclaine in the film 'Sweet Charity'. The cultural icons and attendant others spent the first part of the evening in the local pub, which seemed to have been deliberately and conveniently plonked right at the end of Eric's driveway. We all sat down with our drinks and then after asking my age, George decided that I should be first prize in a game of Pool. A bit later he offered to pay my Dad £2,000 for me and I nearly choked on my Bacardi and Coke. I wanted to have this evening's events beamed over to Higham's Park at once and shout, 'Well, superstars like me, so why not you lot?' I never could understand it.

Our little party then staggered out of the pub, back to the house and adjourned to Eric's game's room where we entertained ourselves on the pinball machines. The guys played billiards and Eric was calling Pattie 'Layla'. With teenage curiosity bubbling up in me I asked George what it had been like to be chased by screaming girls all the time and he replied unhelpfully that, 'It was just the same as not being chased by them'! Er, thanks for that. *'Speaking words of wisdom let it be'.*

Things got a bit iffy because Mum and George's girlfriend didn't hit it off that well. She seemed a bit 'up herself' you might say and she wasn't too amused about the attention I was getting either. I suppose that in her eyes Mum and I were nobodies as opposed to the other four who were quite something in the eyes of the world at large. All concerned were out of it and a slightly no holds barred atmosphere began to prevail, which the aforementioned lady was keen to put a stop to and mum said things along the lines of 'steady on chaps.'

Nevertheless, the night ended far too soon for me who could have quite happily have stayed being admired in famous land for evermore. But as we know, life just isn't like that (for me anyway) and soon enough I was back at home in bed.

Not long after I met Anita at Golders Green Station and we got the 102 bus up to Chingford Hatch. It was snowing heavily when we arrived at Trumans and just as I was brushing the wet from my fake fur collar I saw Johnny Gale again. He acted a bit embarrassed at first but we soon broke the ice and in contrast to the weather outside, we affected a full-scale thaw that evening in the saloon bar of The Horseless Carriage. A rumour began to circulate that he had split up with his girlfriend and once more I dared to hope for him. But again nothing came of it, the dream faded and Highams Park was losing me. But don't despair because other avenues that offered fantasy fulfilment were perilously close at hand.

At school we had read the novel 'Flambards' by K.M. Peyton and as impressionable young girls our romantic appetites were whetted by its anti-hero, Mark Russell. The narrative begins a few years before the outbreak of The First World War and the character of Mark is something akin to a teenage amalgam of the fictional characters of Steerforth and Flashman. He is portrayed as a good looking and arrogant public schoolboy, with just a trace of vulnerability; very much the old school at odds with a modern world. In the follow up novels, he takes on the mantle of the real-life Siegfried Sassoon musing over his foxhunting glories as he becomes 'Mad Jack,' fearlessly striding across no man's land invading German dug outs and dodging machine gun bullets, armed only with a revolver (but not gay). The essential motif of 'Flambards' is that of a rural horsey world, set amongst crumbling mansions looming out of the mist and rook filled elm trees towering over brimming ditches.

By 1976, my father was getting so interested in the game of Polo that he had bought two more horses to add to his existing pair. I had noticed at various social events that there seemed to be a lot of nice men hanging about looking arrogant and well connected. So that February, I started going down to Ham Polo Club with Dad on Sunday mornings, ostensibly 'to help with the horses.' Whoever believed that rubbish is having a laugh but apparently every body did and the grooms urged me to come along more often and learn the ropes. It really did seem like a good idea at the time and I looked upon it as an opportunity to meet rich and interesting males.

Like many of us however, I was totally unaware of just where my rash decision-making was going to lead me. Initially, I really didn't like getting dirty and I was terrified of horses. But I'd truck on down there in old platform boots and spend my time surreptitiously eyeing up this incredibly attractive guy who liked to swan about in a poncho, whilst I half heartedly learnt how to muck out a stable. Now this beautiful man was named Mark and Ham Polo Club was all stark and muddy in its winter splendour. I started to read 'Flambards' again. I was keen to drop the other dreams that I'd now tired of but as usual things have a habit of turning up unexpectedly.

I opened the front door to a smiling Johnny Gale. I had planned a party some time before and The Drunkards had of course been invited. It was John's twenty-fourth birthday and he had come over with a few others all the way from Chingford in a Triumph Herald. He seemed fairly impressed with the house, the giant fish tank (which to take its weight, we had had to have the floor joists strengthened), the quadraphonic stereo system and the gold discs. But I was less than thrilled to see him there I have to say. He certainly noticed my coolness, but I don't think he was too heart broken because he managed to enjoy himself with some other guests. Until my parents arrived back from a night in town and Dad threw them all out into the street for being too noisy in the early hours of the morning. 'And good riddance indeed', I thought as I did the clearing up, 'You've had your chance and I need to get back to Flambards'.

What a coincidence it was that Christina, the teenage heroine of Flambards, had a favourite strawberry roan coloured horse and my Dad had a similar coloured nag that I became very attached to. My life suddenly got very 'Flambardy' indeed as I continued to go down to Ham every weekend and tried to understand this horse thing. And lo and behold! Before you bloody knew it I could muck out single handed, I could pick out feet, I knew which brushes to use in the correct order and I could even stand behind a horse without having heart failure. After a bit of a baptism of fire by Dad who put me straight on the mad horse, which buggered off ('Dad, how do you stop?'), I was having lessons in the top paddock on a quiet mare just like Christina!

I sat my O'levels in between going up to the yard and I whiffed so much that no one would sit next to me. But hey, I was rocking up to chukkas in Richmond Park and going for drinks afterwards with shipping heir Anthony Embiricos, Small Faces drummer Kenney Jones and music impresario Bryan Morrison. One morning Dad and I got up early and went for breakfast at The Royal Lancaster Hotel in London with the Wigdahl brothers. These were a couple of lanky blond polo-playing beauties from across the pond that Dad seemed to want to play some matches with. For the next two weeks my imaginary world consisted solely of deciding which one of these lovelies I would be marrying, but I'm very sad to say that I never ever saw them again.

But I was still seeing lots of Mark who drove an old green Triumph and I was always looking out for that thing, so much so that any green Triumph I saw anywhere would give rise to the hope that Mark may be in it. Of course Mark was well aware that his mate's daughter had a crush on him and I can say that with certainty because we had a party at our place to which he came, without his girlfriend (a person with a Purdey haircut named Annabel). What joy to have him in my house, until Dad announced with gusto that, 'We all know that Nettie fancies Mark.' Thanks.

Then I danced with him at the Ham Ball. I was wearing my Grandmother's 1940s black cocktail dress and he threw the stalk from a carnation down the gap where my cleavage should have been. Nevertheless, because he was about thirty, I knew in my heart that I didn't have a snowball's chance in hell with this one. But I wasn't too down because I managed to have quite a good time with the grooms.

Such as eighteen year-old Abi, a tall girl with a round face and very long brown, centre-parted hair. Abi taught me a lot about horses and we shared a hobby of writing a lot of obscure and silly poetry, which we read to each other. Her poems were interesting to me as they dealt with adult themes like having sweaty sex with men, whilst mine were mainly about failed romance and April showers. Abi would take me out and about with her in the evenings to The Orange Tree pub in Richmond and she had this really appalling friend called something like Andrea who was also eighteen and a bit of a slapper. I think that Andrea quite correctly, surmised that I was a dippy, innocent virgin and she decided that I needed to know a bit more about the birds and the bees. I sat in embarrassed silence whilst she held forth about some mind-boggling porno film exploits she had got up to with two blokes. I was fairly horrified and must have shown it, because she sneered, 'You're not a virgin are you?' at me with barely concealed scorn. I have to admit that at that precise moment in time I was very glad that I was if what she'd been up to was anything to go by!

Abi's busy nightlife didn't interfere too much with her very early mornings at the stables because she had a bit of help in the shape of Amphetamine Sulphate. Now this is a brilliant drug but it would be another eight years at least before I was to be found dabbling in such things. One night however, Abi decided to take me with her to score some speed. I had seen quite a bit of drug taking already with my parents and their friends, but always in a clean and moneyed environment. Therefore, nothing on earth had prepared me for the experience that I was about to have.

We arrived at a seedy and run down squat somewhere in the vicinity of Richmond. It consisted of damp and dark staircases, dirty, broken windows, a frighteningly black hallway and a basement from which there burnt a bright yellow light. A couple of filthy, staring wraiths then appeared from a room in which paint peeled from the walls and a dirty sink lurked in a corner. There was a cat there, which I felt sorry for. I was fully cognisant of my own naivety and thought perhaps I should be feeling pity but mainly I found these monsters both horrifying and pathetic. I came out of that place realising just how very sweet indeed my own life was in comparison. So you may imagine my surprise, when in the mid 1990's I met Abi again and she had become a well-respected member of The Metropolitan Police.

For the early part of 1976, the good life continued and we remained based at Ham. I left school illegally before the summer term began. I say 'illegally', because theoretically I should have stayed on for another year, but I had done my exams and because it was a private school, no one said a word. No one ever mentioned the words 'further education', 'career' or 'university' to me either, but to be fair to them I was at that time dead against being stuck in any institution at all.

It seemed like the best idea in the world to live for today and Dad and I were soon well in with all the polo players and partying on down. One party we went to had a swimming pool that lay inside a giant silver bubble in the garden. This was accessed by means of a large zip, which when opened caused great clouds of steam to billow out into the wintry air of early April. I was wearing a bikini with bottoms that had tie sides and some red-headed bloke called Marcus sidled over and thought it would be a good laugh to untie them. Ha ha. Not. I was quite popular now and again and even though I was a size eight, a wag named Melvin gave me the nickname of 'Botty'.

Dad began playing matches at other clubs and he got fed up with having to pay for Ham's grooms to go with him because he reckoned that they got enough livery out of him as it was. Mum had also been doing the club house flowers and hanging baskets for free. He decided it would be a good idea to have a groom of his own and a large arrow was seen pointing at my head. The first match I did I was so green that I wasn't even allowed to ride down to the lines and had to, puff, puff, walk them down in hand. I still thought I was Christina out of Flambards though, so I didn't appear to mind.

I fell in love with the nags and remember boring Mark's ears off at a party talking about my beloved horse Chamango. We went down to Tidworth for the tournament. Eric (Clapton) came along for a visit and he walked over to me to say, 'Hi' as I sat upon my steed looking mega-capable with two lead horses on either side. Unfortunately for me, Chamango only ever stood still for a free hit during a game of polo. So the laid back image of me nonchalantly leaning over my horse's neck for a bit of small talk with hunky Eric was somewhat marred by the fact that my charger suddenly executed a one hundred and eighty degree turn, leaving me looking very flustered and tangled up in various lead ropes whilst the horses attacked each other. I was mortified to say the least, but animals are a great leveller they say.

At the Officer's Dance, Dad forced me to jive with him as he took the piss out of all the 'chinless wonders' in there.

'God help us if we ever have a war!' He said

There was yet another big party held on the last night of the tournament in a huge Marquee. For some reason that must've seemed like a good idea to *them*, drunken revellers decided to get *on* the tent as opposed to *in* it. I was sitting on my own inside, on a chair, in an inebriated state wondering why nobody loved me, only dimly aware of the mayhem above my head. Suddenly Richard (another groom), rushed in, shouted at me, grabbed my hand and dragged me out, just as the tent collapsed under the weight of a load of writhing maniacs. Quite a good headline that would've been, **'Rock Star's Daughter 15, Crushed in Drunken Polo Tent Horror'**!

What *was* grabbing the headlines however; was the famous 1976 heat wave and the polo field at Ham became baked into a solid and unyielding lump of cracking clay. Dad's favourite horse, Pampero 'the grey', became an early casualty of man's desire to thunder about on rock hard ground. A bone disease undisclosed at the time of purchase (this is normal practice in the world of unknowledgable person buying horse) became latent as a result of the continual concussion and therefore the mad Pampy was with much regret, relegated to the great green pasture in the sky. As the summer wore on the provincial feel of the club, coupled with memories of Pampy, caused

Dad to seek out his own pastures new.

We soon discovered that Cowdray Park in West Sussex was where it was all happening and our horses were moved down to one of the yards at Todham for the end of the season, along with a (very much more experienced) groom from Ham. At Cowdray the heat wave continued to crank the thermostat right up and the wheat fields shone like rippling gold, so I called it 'The Summerland'. One morning at the end of August, I was up about six a.m. and I had to walk a few hundred yards along the baked path through the fields of stubble and down into a sunken lane. The sun climbed in a haze of rose coloured light over the high hedgerows and the breeze blew soft and fragrant. Far away from dusty suburbia, it really was very beautiful indeed and life had a bit of promise about it. Love, riches and glory awaited me of that I was certain. Down at the yard, some idiot (probably me) had left the saddles out and Chamango had made a good job of eating them!

Mind you, I had to stay in some rough (for me) places, which I didn't like. One of these was a grim old hole outside Midhurst, called 'The Bothy'. I came back there late one night and had to grope my way along the walls to find my bed in the pitch black. There was an old Tudor cottage at Todham where I also got plonked. It was really grotty as groom's places often are, sparsely furnished with truckle beds and mouldy carpets. Then Dad got very friendly with the young England polo player Alan Kent and for a while I lived with him and his then girlfriend Sally in their cottage (where she often complained to me about the low standard of my washing up).

As well as getting friendly with most of the grooms, I also made friends with Gig. Gig's real name was Victoria Horswell and she was a sister of the legendary polo playing brothers John and Ed. Gig was a strapping lass, about ten years my senior and she very efficiently ran the horse-side of her family's Polo operation. She took me under her wing, taught me a lot about boring horsey stuff and we had a laugh together. Gig invited me to a house party at the family pad in Gloucestershire, where she put me on a safe old bay mare called Esmerelda and took me out with her along the wide green 'Rides' of Cirencester. At their large stone house it was something akin to a weekend house party of the nineteen-thirties and I was living the 'Flambards' dream indeed. John Horsewell was a tall, broad shouldered, mythic figure with long dark hair and he had his girlfriend staying in his room with him; something that I thought was very liberal. The other male guests consisted of the jockey Martin Brown and Guard's Captain Charlie Graham who were equally attractive and out of my league, but it all added to the memorable status of the occasion. It was terribly spiffing, tally ho and top hole. In the evenings, I wore my Mum's huge Terry De Havilland, striped platform sandals, drank Bucks Fizz by the gallon and Gig succeeded in getting me to eat Brie for the first time in my life.

Back in Sussex, Dad and I got invited swimming a couple of times up at Lord Cowdray's. On one occasion the millionaire Vesety brothers were there. This was before Mark Vestey had his accident and he bounded around the pool in tiny dark trunks, with his sun streaked hair and brown body, looking young, attractive and vital. Sam Vestey said something complimentary to me about my borrowed swimwear (I never had the right gear because with my father you never knew what would happen next) and Dad said jokingly, 'She's jail bait.' I honestly had no idea what he meant by that.

Lord Cowdray lived in the newer Hall up by the House Grounds. But the River Grounds, then as now, were dominated by the towering ruins of old the Cowdray Hall, which stood back from the road just outside Midhurst and had been destroyed by fire in 1793. Nowadays, surprise, surprise, you are forbidden to enter for safety, snore, I've fallen asleep, reasons. But in back in ye good olde 1970's we cared not if we were to be struck on the bonce by falling masonry and the club held barbecues in there. At one such bash, I had decided that I had a crush on the young Ed Horswell with his lovely dark curly hair and vivid blue eyes. But poor Ed began to think 'help me' as they usually did and I began to think 'I'm sad' as I usually did, when the extraordinarily handsome and genuine Charlie Graham came and cheered me up. We did a mock duet to Elton and Kiki's hit 'Don't go Breaking My Heart' and the blue lights played behind the smoke from the barbecue, illuminating the ruins against the night sky like a ghostly re enactment of the conflagration.

Yes Dad and I spent many hours whizzing up and down the winding roads between Harrow and Midhurst and the two Jensens became a regular feature flashing along at high speed and overtaking all the 'worms' (this was the name Dad gave to several cars that were in a line stuck behind a slow one). I believe he whittled his journey time down to something like forty-five minutes, which is going some I can tell you! We would often pop into Eric's as he was on the route. Dad had become very close to Eric and Pattie and he affectionately joined in with their pet names of 'Ello' and 'Nello'. This was a time when EC was drinking quite a bit of brandy and he would sit and watch endless episodes of 'Rising Damp' on his TV, whilst strange people floated about the place. Once I saw Charlotte Martin in the hallway (an ex of Eric's whom we'd known well in the sixties). She looked a bit out of it and was with a longhaired bloke that I only vaguely recognised (this was

Jimmy Page).

Sometimes Dad and I stayed the night there and I was given a bedroom with hippy tapestries draped around its terracotta painted walls and it had a tall window that overlooked the emerald coloured tangle of garden. One night, Eric held a party to celebrate Robert Stigwood's birthday. Not many people were there when Dad and I arrived, so left to my own devices (and some alcoholic beverages) I struck up a conversation with a friendly woman and I started to tell her all about my horses. She very kindly managed not to fall into a stupor of boredom and it wasn't until some years later that I realised (with no little embarrassment) that the person who had so patiently put up with my teenage ramblings was none other than the singer and actress Barbara Dickson. Comedian Frankie Howerd took my hand and read my palm, telling me that I was destined to marry a man 'surrounded by music' (oddly, but not unpredictably correct). However, thrill to end all thrills, guess who turned up amongst some other well-known faces? None other than Elton John himself and I was beside myself with delight to actually encounter in the flesh the person who sang the soundtrack to my life. Dad in an act that was unusual for him, went over and said something to Elton who in turn came over to me and said, 'Hi, I really love your skirt, it's the best at the party.' (I was wearing a tightly pleated, calf-length tartan skirt.) I'm still as pleased as punch to have met him.

Dad had now hooked up with a musician named Benny and he happened to be the adopted son of the world wildlife expert Dr Miriam Rothschild. So when the polo season ended in September, our three remaining horses were boxed up to her estate at Ashton Wold in Northamptonshire. This was an entire village that had been built by her father circa 1900 (a bit like Prince Charles's 'Poundland' or whatever you call it. Can you imagine? 'Any house for a pound'!). Dr Miriam was an extraordinary character and she could usually be seen wearing a headscarf and a flowing skirt with wellies as she drove around her estate in a battered old Bentley. She lived in a large rambling, high-gabled house, complete with a wide, imposing stone terrace that looked out over sloping lawns. It had allegedly had the whole top floor removed at some point because a family member had hanged himself in one of the rooms. In her drawing room, there was an old sepia photograph of her father in command of four zebras harnessed to a carriage. This was an incredible feat apparently, as they are notoriously difficult to handle. When we had dinner there and had finished our meal, she informed us imperiously that, 'We never stack the plates'. Remember that when you need to impress any Aristos that come to dinner.

In order to keep the horses well looked after, Dad had once again snaffled one of the grooms from Ham and she was ensconced, along with her fella, in a tiny, picturesque (but bloody freezing) cottage in the village. We turned the nags out and watched them enjoying their freedom in a field burnt brown and dry from the heat wave. Then suddenly, the weather broke and the heavy rain caused the countryside to green up in a hurry. Dad reckoned that he would be playing the whole of the next polo season at Cowdray Park and I spent the early part of the winter based back at home in Harrow and going up and down to see the horses quite a bit.

Autumn arrived more 'Flambard'-like than ever and sometimes I would go into London to see Gig Horsewell who was helping out in an upmarket, family run arty establishment called The Sladmore Gallery in Bruton

Place. I got a Saturday job at a local greengrocers (Janet also worked there, clue to how I got it). There I sold fruit and veg in brown paper bags to locals including columnist Clare Rayner's unassuming husband and boiled up inky beetroot in a bleak and wintry back yard. Otherwise, I passed the time by reading Lord of the Rings, writing poems about the 'Summerland' and a novel about a rich girl in the nineteen-twenties who gets off with a troubled and handsome devil called... Mark! (Decades later, my daughter had me incoherent with laughter at her less than complimentary comments on that narrative!)

> Bedecked in splendid greenery,
> My Summerland it stands,
> Awaiting me on my return
> From all the winter lands.

The New Year brought a bit of a reality check however, but not one that put me off my stride too badly. Dad had bought three more horses from Lord Patrick Beresford and so he contacted a mad polo-playing mate of his from Nigeria called Colin, who had a house and stables near Windsor Great Park. Colin agreed to have the horses at his place for a while until the season started and in February they had to come in to their stables again to be got fit and ready for polo. Now I wonder who would have to do the mucking out and stuff?? Dad deposited me down at Colin's, where I knew no one and had to sleep in one of his kid's bunk beds (where were they?). I didn't like it at all. The horses were more than I could handle, especially Nino, who unbeknownst to us, had already had four grooms in hospital. Read the chapter in Jilly Cooper's novel 'Polo' that deals with horse abuse and you will know why. Anyway, Nino hated men to such an extent that Dad and Colin couldn't get near him. I was in the kitchen making lunch when two sheepish faces appeared at the window, 'Can you help us?' they said.

I was thrilled to be nominated as person most likely to succeed in getting on the back of the quivering, dangerous and unpredictable nervous wreck. However, Nino did prefer girls and so I survived this perilous experience in the fading light of a winter's afternoon.

In addition to these fun and games, the grooms in the wilds of Ashton Wold decided that due to lack of funds they would execute a moonlight flit. Instead of leaving the quadrupeds in the paddock, they (perhaps on purpose?) left the nags in their stables, which meant that we had to get there fast. Snow lay deep in the fields on either side of the road as we raced through the night up the A1 and the sun rose like an orange orb through the frozen mist. Everywhere the world appeared barren and desolate, with miles of barbed wire fencing and empty branches black against the snow that was now stained pink by the onset of the dawn.

Once at the cottage, we couldn't even make a cuppa as they'd taken everything including the light bulbs! The furry, fat nags though were luckily none the wiser. From this moment on, a silly time ensued which involved travelling merrily up and down the A1 (Sandy, Stilton, Peterborough), looking after the two sets of horses. *'3-5-7-9 little white line, motorway sun coming up with the morning light.'*('2-4-6-8 Motorway':Tom Robinson)

Inevitably, I would get dumped at either place and once Anita came and stayed with me. But wherever I was, I was nearly always frozen solid, miserable and lonely. Surely this never happened in Flambards?

CHAPTER FIVE
Jilly Cooper's Polo: 1977

If anyone ever asks me, in reference to the above mentioned novel, 'Was it really like that in Polo?' the answer is always a resounding, 'Yes!'

The only difference being that whilst everyone else was having sex everywhere I most assuredly was not, even though I was now sixteen and legal. Dad rented us our own yard that year within easy hacking distance of the polo grounds in the sleepy West Sussex village of Lodsworth. We managed to gather the disparate nags together including the three from Beresford, one of which had to go back due to a (money related?) problem. She had been lovely and 'normal' as opposed to the other two liabilities that I got lumbered with looking after. Okay, I did quite like them, but Piggy was an unrideable maniac with a mouth like cast iron (no brakes) and Nino, as we know, was a terrified and dangerous jelly on legs more in need of a behavioural therapist than a groom.

The yard was pleasantly situated and was owned by a couple called Beard (Jimmy Hill, no relation). Mr Beard had several vintage cars secreted in his barns and he never took them out anywhere that I noticed. The Beard's stipulated that we must use peat for bedding, which left our bored horses with nothing to chew on to pass the time and the useless grooms (was one of them me?) more often than not forgot to put muzzles on them (well, I thought it was cruel). The result of this was, that by the end of the season, Chamango and Chrissy had just about eaten through the central pillar supporting the roof and Mango also ate the wood holding his top door on, so that it fell off into the yard just as Mr Beard walked by. Ooops!

In the early part of the season, I spent a lot of time with the grooms down at Todham and they took me along to The Cowdray Park point-to-point. They were obviously a lively lot as it was in their cottage that I noticed these semi-porn mags called Forum, which were an eye-opener for me I must say. But on a less alarming note, I was with them on Grand National Day and we all screamed and cried at the telly with genuine emotion as we watched Rummy in his sheepskin noseband come in for the third time.

The first groom that we got to help us was an army chap from up north. He was a blond with a bowly haircut and glasses and we called him 'Yorkshire Terry'. Nino hated him so much that he got down on the sand track in order to remove him, so I had to ride him after that. Then I fell off Nino on the golf course and Terry fell off his horse. The two steeds could be seen silhouetted against the sky wearing full tack but no riders and Dad went apoplectic. Alan Kent very kindly took me to hospital and nothing was broken so the hospital staff took my wheelchair away and made me hop out. The tough and respected grooms like Mel up at Todham, said I was too crap a rider to handle such a nutty nag as Nino, which made me all the more determined to do so. The great Australian ten-goal player Sinclair Hill gave me some fine advice and I was soon riding Nino about like a little dobbin. (Lord Beresford stood amazed at one match, unable to recognise his former mental patient.)

At a yard barbecue, Terry got thrown into a water trough by fellow revellers. Unperturbed, he pretended to be having a bath and used his empty beer bottle as a loofah. Together we would hack down to the polo grounds in glorious weather, taking three horses apiece and singing loudly to the radio that Terry had secreted somewhere about his person. Down at the River Grounds, under the shady trees, you would see the Cowdray horses coming along in their orange bandages exactly as Ms Cooper describes them. And at Ambersham, we'd pass the Harper greys, wending their weary way homewards. Their legs and backs stained pink with the dye from their bright red saddle-cloths and bandages.

We then acquired a horse called Big Boy that would never go on the lorry. Once, John Horswell blind folded him with a coat. Another time four of them carried him in backwards and on yet another occasion Sinclair Hill himself rode him fearlessly up the ramp. We were always late if we had to take him anywhere, which after one match resulted in him being left behind at Cirencester until someone mustered the time and effort to go back for him. (This was the weekend that Mum and Dad ran out of petrol on their way to Stevie Winwood's place which was nearby. They had to push the Jensen into someone's driveway and walk the five miles to Stevie's. This caused them to miss a party of Eric's that they were supposed to go to that night. 'I wondered why there was a Jensen in my garden' said the baffled resident the next day). However, on one match day, I ordered the lorry two hours early to be on the safe side, brought the naughty horse out and warned the driver that he wouldn't load. He walked straight up. Never did it again though.

In the meantime, the pace was hotting up and in order to mount a team and replace those animals that went lame, we were getting new horses by the minute; as well as travelling to away matches and attending every party going. We went off to Tidworth where we had such dashing hunks as John Horswell, Charlie Graham, Gonzo Pierez and Hector Crotto playing for our team, The Dragonflies. The horses were decked out in green bandages and had green and white brow bands.

'There is no finer sight,' said Dad 'than that of seeing my horses coming along to a match in my team colours.'

We won the tournament easily despite all the players being hung over from carousing the night before. There is no finer sight, say I, than that of tired and sweaty young men limping along attired in tight, dirty white breeches and long leather boots.

We also won the Rutland cup for the second year running and then headed up to Lincolnshire to trounce another lot. Us grooms got money and we gulped champagne out of the silver trophy. Then we swigged wine and sang loudly all the way back in the lorry, much to the consternation of the poor driver. I spent many hours sitting in horseboxes, swinging through sunny, shabby council estates on the outskirts of endless rural towns and villages. Watching the locals buying their weekend papers from corner shops and grubby half naked children running across the road holding dripping ice-lollies. The noise of the engine would drown out the occasional sounds of horses kicking and neighing, whilst I ate crisps and breathed in the twin scents of dung and diesel.

Back at Cowdray, I was busy at the pony lines on match days, longingly awaiting the arrival of the tea trolley that was filled with sandwiches and cakes. Nino in particular enjoyed oranges and ham sandwiches, which I would share with him until Dad caught me, 'Will you stop feeding that fucking horse chocolate cake before I've played him.' Then he would fly into the lines on Piggy or the chestnut gelding Colibri, unable to slow down after a chukka, shouting, 'Will you stop you bastard!' whilst hoiking the beast hard in the mouth to virtually no effect whatsoever, sending panicked grooms and horses scattering in all directions. I would be waiting at the edge of the pitch to grab the reins of the sweaty, blowing maniac he'd just played, which would then circle madly around me as I held an anxious fresh horse for him to get on, settle him in and hand him his stick. If I accidentally gave the wrong sized stick I'd get hit on the head with it, 'I said a fucking 52 you idiot!' Ouch!

At chukkas at The House Grounds, our young horse Project escaped and went for a jog over Lord Cowdray's croquet lawn. Dad got really worried that he'd be in for a bollocking and sheepishly set off through the trees to reclaim his wayward nag.

'Fine young horse that Ginger!' exclaimed Lord C from his terrace, and went down to help Dad catch him. We lent our young thoroughbred mare Chrissy, to the Canadian Russell Corey for the '77 Gold Cup. Young 'Baggins' as we called her, was an ex-racehorse and she helped the team to victory, galloping towards goal several yards ahead of her nearest rival.

When I was still at school, Sheryl had got me into reading historical romances such as 'The Legend of The Seventh Virgin' by Victoria Holt. She then turned me on to Anya Seaton's novel 'Green Darkness', which is a time travelling romance set in... Midhurst. So 'Flambards' was slightly out the window now as I discovered the mysterious and romantic environs of this beautiful West Sussex town and hoped that romance was surely just around the corner. For a while, Dad and I stayed at The Angel Hotel on the main drag. I used to sit in my room in the evenings and watch 'Rock Follies' on a little black and white TV. In the mornings, a young male member of the hotel staff would bring me in a cup of tea (sent by Dad to make sure I got up) and one day he asked me out. Help and no thanks. What? with all those polo players about?

I spent a lot of time in The Half Moon pub just outside of the town, and this was the haunt of 'The Blond Bombshells'. This was a term used by the female grooms to describe Howard and Julian Hipwood, Sandy Harper, Johnny Kidd (father of Jodie, Gemma and Jack) and Oliver Ellis. Not forgetting the dark-haired beauties, the Horswells and Charlie Graham. These were indeed good days to be alive. We stayed and socialised at Alan's and at Oli's. We played bar billiards and ate basket meals in The White Horse at Graffham (where my mother once hit me on the head with a pool cue). But unfortunately it was only the tarty Argies (like Eddie the gorgeous groom with the red beret) who seriously propositioned me and even then I was able to work out that they were a waste of time.

During Gold Cup week things got madder than ever and up in 'tent city' where all the visiting grooms had their temporary quarters, it was universally agreed that on a good night you could actually see the caravans rocking. I have it on good authority that one notorious Argy groom swore by regular doses of a horse tonic to improve his stamina and that consequently he was later discovered to be the source of an outbreak of the clap that raged through the polo community, uniting both players and grooms alike in an orgy of pre-AIDS sleaze. Maybe I didn't miss out on much after all.

Meanwhile, other scandals were doing the rounds. There was Sandy Harper arm in arm with Dudley Moore's ex-wife Suzy Kendall and Hector and Susan Barrantes were recently back on the scene after her parting from Ronnie Ferguson. My Dad liked Ron and I got quite friendly with his vivacious daughter Sarah, who was keen to know which icons of the rock world I had met. She would ring me sometimes for a gossip when I was at home in Harrow and she thought I constantly had super stars coming round for tea. Come to think of it, George Harrison did turn up at least once for a cuppa and I well remember Eric sitting cosily in our lounge and asking us to turn the telly over because a programme about a woman giving birth was putting him off his beans on toast!

Also back in Harrow, they were having a street party down in Littleton Crescent in honour of HM's Silver Jubilee year (and over in Higham's Park dear old Truman's Sports Ground got re-named 'Jubilee' in its honour). I made patriotic hats for my small siblings and Johnny Ball came to entertain us. My sister was invited up to sing a song that went on for so long that the organisers felt it prudent to have her tactfully removed. Then my brother got up and recited the version of 'Row, Row Row your Boat' that ends with the line, *'Throw your teacher over board and listen to her scream'.*

In the evening, we had fireworks that Dad had ordered from Brocks and the task fell to him to let them off. The crowd stood far too close however and our next-door neighbour Jo Hansford (of hairdressing fame), had her neck burnt by a stray rocket, which put a damper on things. She made it clear that she intended to sue Brocks over the incident and my Dad was not amused about it. He was also pretty scathing about The Sex Pistols sailing up the Thames and the reason he wasn't keen on them was because, 'They can't play their instruments.' (Ironic when you consider that he later played on the great John Lydon's 1986 PiL album 'Rise')

Then I had my first encounter with a real live Punk.

Janet knew a bloke who lived down the road called Mick and he had a mate called Mark. Janet and I were round at Mick's when they introduced us to this friend of theirs known as 'Punk William'. Now Punk William looked very extraordinary indeed to my unaccustomed eyes. He was all straight lines and sharp hair, as opposed to the usual floppy fringes and flappy flares (though we were also wearing 'drainpipes' now occasionally). He was raving about The Sex Pistols and he told us that we simply *must* listen to them. With great ceremony he put the single onto the record deck, truly believing that we would all become immediately enlightened. If only it were that simple. My ears were unable to process the sound that came out of the speakers into anything recognisable that could enter my brain. That's how different it was. Poor William, I'm sorry to say that I just dismissed him as being mad.

I wasn't really in any position to go off as an anti-royal family campaigner at that time anyway, because I was attending the same functions as its members. My parent's and I were invited to Lord Cowdray's Ball to which I wore a Thea Porter dress of Mum's, made of crocus yellow satin and edged with purple velvet. The puffed chiffon sleeves were slashed from shoulder to wrist, terminating in long buttoned cuffs and on my feet I wore a pair of emerald glitter Terry De Havilland shoes that I'd bought from his Chelsea shop back in 1975. Sounds awful, but it wasn't.

Even though it was supposed to be black tie, Dad got away with wearing a bottle green suit with a cravat and Mum wore a black and green creation with a floaty skirt and a top that was laced tightly up the front. We arrived at the front of Cowdray Hall in the silver Jensen and a flunkey immediately appeared to park it for us. Once inside, we were confronted by the spectacle of the beautifully dressed, the rich and the well connected, all displayed to great advantage in ornate gilded mirrors and under glittering chandeliers. Charlie Graham bounced over to me looking stunning in a white Tux. He said he thought he looked like an ice-cream waiter, then he asked me to dance. We were both amused by the fact that although I'd got loads of ballroom dancing medals from my school days, I'd always had to be the man because I was tall. Therefore, when we began to Waltz, Charlie kept whispering, 'You're leading, you're leading, why are you leading? Stop it!' So I had to concentrate on going backwards. Suddenly, Charlie started speaking like a ventriloquist and muttering behind his teeth, 'Look there he is! Over there!' and he manoeuvred me across the dance floor until I practically crashed into Prince Charles who was dancing with the anorexic looking Sarah Spencer. *'God Save The Queen'.*

Mum and I were having a whale of a time and could easily have stayed longer, but no, Dad had a match the next day and was hassling us to go home. In the morning, there I was once more headed for Cowdray but this time in the scruffy attire of a polo groom and naturally I was feeling a bit tired. Dad leaned over from the driving seat and handed me a small blue pill, 'Take this' he said. I think it was a Dexedrine designed to make sure that your groom doesn't nod off on the job; but I don't remember that it had any effect on me whatsoever.

Another party that Dad and I went to was up in the wilds of Leicestershire. It was a sort of Deb's ball for the daughter of this upper crust woman who appeared to have some kind of drug connection. On the way there we were stopped by the police. They informed us that there was a dangerous escaped convict on the loose and to be extra vigilant. He was probably already at the party. I was wearing my wonderful tartan skirt and a tartan jumper, with knee length burgundy stiletto heeled boots. Once there I was informed in no uncertain terms that as usual my attire was incorrect and that they would supply me with something more appropriate.

The well-spoken daughter urged me to put on a most hideous navy blue, red edged, puffed sleeved, multi-layered, tent-like concoction, which I did grudgingly in order to restore peace and sanity to the proceedings. The party was in full swing when I reappeared down the main staircase looking like one of those dolls they put over toilet rolls and it was filled with several Argy polo players with whom I was familiar (but not that familiar). Lord Cowdray's son Charlie Pearson was also there and he asked me to dance. (I had got quite friendly with Charlie and his sister Rosie at Cowdray.) Whilst I was dancing with Charlie a cheeky Argy cut in, not that I noticed much because as usual I had had one over the eight, or eighteen more like. Somehow I ended up in the car park, in a car, getting off with a young bloke whose name I most certainly cannot remember. Then things started to get a bit too friendly for my liking, so I decided to call it a day and escaped back inside where a breakfast of egg and bacon, kedgeree and devilled kidneys was already being served. How jolly civilised I say.

For some reason, Dad believed that Charlie Pearson really liked me and the fact that he was heir to an absolutely enormous fortune might have had something to do with him being so keen on the idea. In all fairness to Charlie, I have to say that he never once made any suggestion whatsoever about seeing me. However, that didn't stop Dad from nearly having a fit when I did actually find a boyfriend down at Cowdray. His name was Ray Dixon, he was nineteen years old and he was the Groundsman's son. Then Dad also went down market and began a dalliance with one of the grooms; a girl named Kat. Kat was only about seventeen (ooeer), and she lived in the sleepy village of Woolbeding with her parents.

Without further ado and I presume with some sort of financial agreement, I was living there too. Heaven alone knows what these parents thought about all this? I have no idea because to me there was nothing odd about it. Anyway, I was going out with Ray and one of his mates was the local milkman named Bernie ('*and he drove the fastest milk cart in the west*'). There was a little two-way cupboard off the kitchen where Bernie left the milk and we would leave silly notes for each other in there. Ray came from a huge family and many of them got their livings from the working end of polo. (One of his sisters was a groom who had lost part of her finger when a lead horse had bolted and she had unwisely had the rope wrapped around her hand.) With Ray I experienced a bit more of the normal world.

We cruised the pubs of Midhurst and he took me to football parties where he drunkenly sang '*come on you blues*' with his arms around a bunch of mates. Sometimes, I would go to watch him play cricket and he clowned about to get my attention whilst he was fielding. I dyed my hair red and I got very thin indeed and went down to six and a half stone. Ray said that if I turned sideways and stuck my tongue out I'd look like a zip. But by August our innocuous little romance was over because I caught him flirting with some girl at a party. Is that all? I was still angling for a polo player if truth be told.

Dad's fling with Kat was also on the wane, but I did like her up until the time Dad bought her a really nice pair of pale blue suede, lace-up Terry De Havilland ankle boots and wouldn't get me a pair. Then one day Kat took Chrissy, the ex-racehorse, for a gallop on the Roughs and fell off. The horse kicked her in the face and broke her cheekbone, which had to be fixed with wire. Unfortunately, for some reason the wire stuck to her flesh causing her cheek to pucker, which no doubt became a sad reminder of her encounter with the Bakers.

By August we had a new groom called Judith, who was installed with me in a caravan on the yard at Lodsworth. This caravan was fairly dilapidated and infested with earwigs, which got into everything; in the beds, in the orange juice, yuk, yuk, yuk. And that is where I was when the news came over the radio that Elvis was dead. The DJ Annie Nightingale came down and did a big interview for one of the nationals and the press photographed Leda, Judith, Dad and I, all looking thoughtful and standing in a sunny paddock as our horses grazed around us. We took Charlie Graham with us to a party one night that was held on a man made island in the middle of a lake. To reach this place you had walk through a concrete tunnel, the entrance of which was on the shore. As we came up onto the island via a spiral staircase, strains of music floated out across the water, stars sparkled up above and a bubble machine blew its fragile orbs out into the surrounding darkness.

Next up Dad met a bloke named Roy. Roy was at this time the manager of The Petworth Park Hotel. Though how he got that job I've no idea, because he had done a stretch at Her Majesty's pleasure for being apprehended whilst driving the getaway car in an armed robbery (remember not to employ him on your next bank job). We stayed there for a while until there was a row about who was supposed to pay for it. Things were obviously not good between my parents around this time (were they ever?) and this became apparent when I sat in Dad's room there one day as he unpacked his polo things in order to get changed prior to a game. As he took his pristine white breeches from out of his bag, we noticed that my mother had written the word 'CUNT' in large black letters all the way down one leg.

But apart from brief funny moments such as that, my life continued to be devoid of any action and I began to realise that the 'me and a polo player' scenario just wasn't going to happen. I began writing another novel about a well to do eighteenth-century girl who gets kidnapped by a hunky highwayman and falls in love with him (I *had* been reading a lot of Georgette Heyer!). At the same time, life at home when we were there began to show the unmistakeable signs that the glue was starting to seriously come off the wrapping.

CHAPTER SIX
Mr Blue Sky: 1978

The unholy trinity of drug addiction, infidelity and financial worries would spell trouble for any marriage and my parents were no exception. It is not a secret that Dad had battled with heroin since the summer I was conceived, but it wasn't until I was sixteen that the full extent of what such an addiction entailed really came home to me. On many occasions when he took me out I was lumbered with a companion who had 'nodded off' into his soup and this was at the very least embarrassing if nothing else. However, when I shared a room with him once after Polo tournament and he became extremely ill, my eyes were finally opened to the enormity of the problem.

Dad had always had girlfriends and I got on with them because they were nice to me and I never saw anything unusual in it either, but obviously my mother did. My parents had physically fought each other for as long as I could recall and their fights included beating each other with lumps of wood whilst naked (!) and mother throwing a portable paraffin stove at him when it was still alight (he ran). As a small child in Neasden, I was sitting in the garden one day, when a plate of meat and two veg came flying out of the back door onto the lawn. But far, far, worse was having to share a bedroom with them throughout the early nineteen-sixties, which was an experience to say the least. Things very quickly arrived at the smashing stage with those two and extremely violent arguing, year in year out, was normal.

But it was the money thing that really put the lid on it. Polo was a hobby that he just could not afford (hardly anyone can) and Mum was keen to tell him so. She wanted to spend cash on extending the house and having a second bathroom installed and inevitably this was another issue that led to fighting. Yet I never thought for one moment that the cry of, 'We have no money' actually meant just that!

1978 therefore, was the year in which the decline of our fortunes gradually became apparent. In late '77 we wintered the horses at a place in Charville Lane, Hayes. This involved living at home again in the war zone and with my seventeenth birthday approaching I was relying on Janet to get me out and about. Janet had started seeing a lively bloke called Sean and on Christmas Eve she asked me to come down to The John Lyon pub at the bottom of Sudbury Court Drive to meet him. Sean was every bit as eccentric as promised and he had lots of friends who were all aged around nineteen or twenty. Derek 'the Fireman', Dave 'the policeman' (who both went out and got Kevin Keegan curly perms), Brett, Pete, Brian, Gem, Cliff, Noel, Ted, Donna, Caroline & Steve and his brother Tim, to name but a few. Hey presto! I had a new crowd and a new pub to escape to that was almost literally on my doorstep.

On New Years Eve, I went with them to a party where for some inexplicable reason I fell for a complete wanker that they all knew. He had got into a fight and started crying, so I felt sorry for him and looked after him a bit. This person, whom I later discovered to be a certified loon (and it's a shame they never warned me), became for a short and troubled period my boyfriend and the first person with whom I actually did 'it'! On the evening of our first date, early in the New Year, Janet had gone out to a local disco where she happened to overhear his sister bragging loudly, 'Guess who my brother's going out with?' But for the moment I *was* happier and had begun to wonder again if 'normal' life as opposed to the whirl of the polo scene might be worth another try.

And this seemed even more like a good idea as the start of the new season hove into view; because Dad had decided that we were going to go back up to Miriam's to start our own Ashton Wold Polo Club. This was to be in conjunction with the terrible and infamous Luis Basualdo (who had been married to Lord Cowdray's elder daughter and later had a well-documented liaison with Christina Onassis). Now this latest twist didn't appeal to me at all because where were all the hunky players, the parties and the exciting happenings? They certainly were not in the wilds of Ashton Wold.

First of all, I had to stay in this very beautiful but isolated thatched cottage, right on the edge of the village, surrounded by six tall, soughing fir trees. This sinister place had a strange and lonely atmosphere, which may have been due to the fact that some years before, an entire family had been hacked to death there by a mad axe man who had never been caught. It was known locally as 'Murder Cottage'. As usual, it was cold there and when I'd been away I would return to find mouse droppings in my bed. In fact the mice were so hungry there, that they even ate bars of soap, so Dad bought two little kitties to eat the mice and cheer me up.

It *was* a God forsaken place and the surrounding countryside consisted of miles of depressing, flat, open fenland. The old marshes, though drained for centuries now, seemed reluctant to let go of their dark memories of Hereward the Wake and his guerrillas. I'm sure that their ghosts were still hiding out there amongst the Will o' the Wisps whose ghostly candles were said to lure the unwary to their doom. We attended a party that was held in an old Norman manor house in the village of Massingham and the celebrations were further enlivened when the ceiling fell in.

After a short while we moved again, this time to the nearby village of Polebrook. A spot so deathly quiet that my Aunt and Uncle renamed it, 'The Village of the Damned' on a subsequent visit. We rented a farmhouse and stables. The kitties came with us, but eventually one of them moved in with another family and sadly the other one came to grief on the road. Highfields Farm was situated on the left hand bend of the road, just as you entered the village and it was also dare I say it, sparsely furnished, shabby and bloody freezing. Dad had now begun to drink heavily and I would come down in the morning to discover that all the furniture had been overturned and that he had drawn a stick man on the inside of the kitchen door into which he had been throwing knives. Not surprising then that I wasn't all that keen on staying there but it got better when we found someone else to help.

At first we had a groom called Kate Palmer who was the daughter of former Cream roadie (& friend) Ben. Kate wore a leather jacket, smoked roll ups and drank pints; a concept I found intriguing to say the least and I was a bit disapproving. She tried to enlighten me as regards the new ethos that was emerging from young people at the time, but I was having none of it. After Kate, we got a very knowledgeable horse person called Brigitte. We became friends and discovered that there was some life in the village if you looked hard enough. For as luck would have it, over the road was a pub and next door to that was a cottage that was inhabited by three dark-haired brothers between the ages of seventeen and twenty-three.

But before Brigitte arrived I would often escape back to Harrow to have some laughs with The John Lyon crew. One night, the lads set fire to a motor in the car park of The John Lyon. This was for insurance purposes and then they all came back to my house acting mysteriously and stinking of smoke (I won't tell you whose car it was, because his Mum still believes that it caught fire by accident). The Loony (boyfriend) took me to see the film 'Star Wars' at The Empire, Leicester Square. Nowadays it's hard to convey the excitement that was generated by the innovative special effects. But to sit there in 1978 and feel the great whoosh, as the space ship looms overhead in the opening scene, was (in my opinion) to experience a truly ground-breaking moment. On my ticket he wrote romantically, 'Fly into hyperspace with me.' Little did I know that he was already out there!

He was strange to say the least and our evenings out together often ended in disaster. After having a terrible row with him at a disco in Stanmore, our friend Pete threw us his keys and said we could sit in his Ford Zodiac that was parked outside. But The Loony (who had no licence), decided to take the old car for a drive. On the return trip we got stuck in the car park of The Hare pub up in Old Redding because he seized the gearbox whilst attempting to get it into reverse. The two of us managed to hitch a lift home at around one in the morning, but predictably enough, when Pete discovered what had taken place he went mad. My Mum joined forces with him and they scoured the local streets in tandem, intent on hastening The Loony's demise. They never found him though, because he was in fact hiding on our conservatory roof the whole time and I was secretly passing him supplies out of the window.

Meanwhile, Janet and Sean were having a lively time of it as Janet was seeing other people. Janet is one of those very beautiful girls that always seem to have men crawling along the floor and committing suicide over them. Everyone it seemed was wildly in love with her and as her best mate I was always the go between. Why can't *I* have them hanging from trees outside the window and crying in the garden eh? It always made me very cross. I was still seeing a lot of Anita, and she was having a thing with Pete. Pete lived on East Lane in North Wembley and as you may have gathered, he had a mania for old Ford Zodiacs, several of which were parked outside his house. (Later on, he got an American Ford Cutlass and he loved that, but sadly the chassis collapsed when he drove too fast over a pothole in Edgware on his way back from Anita's.) Then Sean started seeing Anita to get Janet riled up. Janet and Anita had already clashed over a member of The Horseless Carriage crew in '75, so it all got a bit heated.

On St George's day we had James Hunt as our celebrity guest down at the pub and we were also treated to Janet roaring into the car park in her burgundy Mini in order to snatch Sean away from Anita. As well as this, Janet and I had also (in our spare time) managed to snaffle two young (younger than us) brothers of some female friends of ours for a secret dalliance. I had Phil and she had Darren. Then I decided to hold a party in our garage, which I mistakenly believed to be a good venue to ensure that there was no damage. Unfortunately, I was ill upstairs with a non-alcohol related complaint (for a change) and a very attractive ballerina friend of mine got off with The Loony. So I went down and thumped him and the evening culminated with Sean fighting Darren over the bonnet of the silver Jensen. For a *grande finale* they hurtled into the wall in the front garden, which collapsed as a result.

Once Brigitte the groom arrived, she came to stay in Harrow one weekend (who was doing the horses?) and a group of us went up to a disco at The Traveller's Rest in Kenton. Brian, who worked for The Gas Board, amused himself by telling all the girls that he was an airline pilot and I'm sure that they believed him. Meanwhile, a fight broke out in the bar and we stood on chairs in order to cheer them on and get a better look. The struggle roared towards the disco area and for a moment they turned the lights on and the music off, but no, it was gone again towards the bar area. The music came back on, '*ah, ah, ah, ah, staying alive, staying alive*', it was all Saturday Night Fever in those days. Suddenly, the fight reappeared having gathered great momentum and a hundred extra brawlers in its temporary absence. Girls were in there too, chairs were flying about, and this huge seething mass was heading straight towards us! '*And the man at the back said 'everyone attack, it's going to turn into a ballroom blitz.*" (Ballroom Blitz: Sweet).

In panic, we heaved the windows up and clambered into the street where we ran for our lives. The fight spilled out onto the pavement behind us, and drunken maniacs brandishing broken bottles, continued to chase each other up and down the Kenton Road as we hastily made our getaway.

Several of us went out and bought ELO's 'Out of the Blue' LP and Mr Clit Westwood himself, aka Sean, certainly did wish he was a 'Wild West Hero' and that Janet was his '*western girl round the fire oh so bright*'. One Saturday morning, a bunch of us piled into Pete's Zodiac for a trip to Bushey Breakers where Sean nicked a part for his car and made me hide it under my coat. It was a glorious April day, the sun was shining and we had 'Mr

Blue Sky' blasting out of the speakers. As we came round a bend in the road, we saw a couple of punks walking along. They had Mohicans, safety pins, the lot. The lads all leaned out of the windows and screamed abuse at them as we roared past, 'What do you fucking look like? What a state!' etc, etc.

I thought they looked fantastic. They epitomised a reckless freedom, giving us the finger as we sped upon our way. We were just a bunch of 'Wedgies' after all, and what did I look like with my flicked up hair do and flowery, long waisted tops?

Quite soon, my own very lame attempt at romance went down the tubes and then I was often to be found crying in *his* garden. The Loony was quite obviously embarrassed by my odd looks, because he named me 'Plug', after the goofy looking character in the Beano comic. He banned me from eating peanut butter as he said it squelched through my front teeth like toothpaste and he said that there was something wrong with me, but that he was too kind to tell me what it was (answers on a postcard please). He would often be playing the Hall and Oates' song 'Rich Girl' very loudly when I arrived at his house, *'You can rely on the old man's money'.* And it would be blasting down the stairs, unpleasant in its implied criticism, whenever I turned up.

One night, the crew decided to go for a late night swim at Harrow School's famous pool 'The Ducker.' We broke in by climbing over the fence and as I jumped down, my eighteen carat gold chain and large filigree Agadez cross that Dad had bought me from West Africa, got caught on the wire and pinged off into the undergrowth. We all spent ages looking for it and never found it. But some years later I was informed by an individual who had been with us that night, that The Loony had in fact found it himself, kept schtum and then flogged it. I never understood why he was so horrible to me when I liked him so much, but I began to know that many more changes lay directly dead ahead.

> *'....I tried my best all I could do,*
> *but somehow it was not enough for you...*
> *..I've been thinking it over, think I'm going to*
> *have to start again, and its rather sad*
> *Because I've looked around, can't seem to find*
> *whatever's always rolling through my mind.*
> *I remember the dead of night,*
> *the lonely light that shines upon the window*
> *I see it all so clear, the tenderness, the silent tears.*
> *Out here in the pouring rain, through cold dark waiting*
> *days I see you standing there,*
> *I see the big wheels turning,*
> *never ending, on and on they go'*
> ('Big Wheels': ELO).

Whilst in Harrow, I forgot my troubles by whizzing up Sudbury Court Drive on the back of Tim's 700 cc Honda motorbike. Then I went back to Polebrook where a team of us hung out now and again at a disused airfield. There was a guy there who had a withered arm from a previous bike accident and he changed gear (or worked the throttle) by moving his shoulder; but I happily tasted some more speed as the pillion on his Kawasaki 650.

Earlier in the spring, father had become friendly with a girl connected to the hunting crowd and she arrived at the stables one-day to clip our horses for us. Over a drink in the local pub that evening she explained to me that the fox-hunting fraternity were in her words, 'Hunting all day and humping all night.' Mr B himself even went out with

The Fitzwilliam Hunt as Master's guest, dressed inappropriately enough, in jeans and an anorak. He rode Project and came back absolutely horrified at the way in which they disregarded their horse's welfare by cantering on the tarmac roads and galloping hell for leather through deep plough. He wasn't impressed.

Eventually the time came to attempt to stage a polo match or two in a field at Ashton Wold. There were no proper polo grooms about so the Argies that were 'on hire,' would request me for games and ask me to bandage the legs of something like twenty horses at a time, because no one else present knew how to do it. But often I could only be enticed back from Harrow if I was allowed to bring a friend for moral support. The first time that this happened, I took Katie (a friend of Janet's), with me, whom Dad tried and (unusually for him), failed to get off with. On the next occasion (and it did seem like a grand idea), I brought the loud, quirky, brown-eyed, myopic, attractive, very skinny, former girlfriend of Sean and a lot of other people. She also just happened to be that star struck sister of The Loony. The rest as they say is history. She it was who was destined to become the person we all refer to as 'Wife number 2', or more usually, 'Number 2'. One of my Mum's mates happened to be up at the polo that Sunday and saw (the not yet) Number 2 sitting on Dad's lap in the pub and although in fact not a lot at all had happened she decided to blow the gaff. Now the (nearly) Number 2 had (being then on friendly terms and a frequent visitor to our house) borrowed Mum's wellies for the trip and when she stood at our front door in Harrow and said, 'Thanks for lending me your boots' Mum replied, 'Yeah, and I hear I lent you my old man as well.'

But life went on in pretty much the same haphazard

way as it had done and before Brigitte the groom and I fully got to grips with the brothers Owen across the way, we managed to meet and go out with another couple of brothers who happened to live in the nearby village of Lutton. My conquest was called Kevin and we did it in the hay barn. These two lads played some instruments after a fashion and would come up to the house when Dad had his drums set up and they'd all jam together. Things were going swimmingly until one day Kev went to see his girlfriend and Brig's blokey went to see his wife. Obviously things then took on a more complicated angle and before long that was the end of that.

So it was onwards and upwards for Brig and I as we checked out the dishy brothers over the road. Brigitte was soon firmly attached to the best looking and oldest brother named Kieron and with them and the other two brothers I walked along the country footpaths that led through the crop fields to The Chequered Skipper pub in Ashton Wold. Initially, the younger brother Julian was interested in me, but one sultry afternoon I got tired of his attentions and set off alone across the stubble. The sound of a motorbike engine cut through the heat haze as it got nearer to me and there was the dishy middle brother Max offering me a lift. Max made a play for me by saying that he 'loved' me (yes we believe you) and he gave me slushy song lyrics on bits of paper. Although he was rather nice, I was reluctant because I imagined that I was still in love (or obsessed) with the Loony. But Max bade me to follow the advice of Steven Stills, who urged in song, *'If you can't be with the one you love, honey, then love the one you're with.'*

On Sunday's, Max and I would go to a pub called The Angel. He had a mate called Billy Bragg and Billy was the singer in a band called 'Riff Raff'. I became a fan and even had a Riff Raff badge ('My Side was a Write Off' is a great song). The bass player was an older guy called Ruan and we renamed him 'Ruin'. They had a single out called 'I am a Cosmonaut' as opposed to an 'Anarchist' I presume? Billy often appeared at the farm after that to see dad, for reasons unknown to me.

Riff Raff managed to get a good gig as a support act in nearby Peterborough, so Max and I went along to see them. The Skids were also on as support and The Stranglers were headlining. This was nothing at all like Baker Gurvitz Army at The Rainbow, as you may imagine. A punk gig in '78, quite cool eh? Not that I thought so at the time. Yes, Riff Raff were great, but the Skid's with Jobson in and Stuart Adamson gyrating around wearing a skintight pink spandex cat suit; what's happening? As for the audience, spiky hair, black make-up and so much gobbing that The Strangler's guitarist was begging them to stop because it was getting all over his strings and he couldn't play. I was, to be honest, shit scared and couldn't wait to get home. In the car it was like being stuck in 'Night of the Living Dead' with zombies all around us. Shame.

But when Number 2 left briefly over some disagreement, Dad got upset and on a visit to Chelsea he picked up a little punk girl whom he brought back with him. I was most impressed with her attire, in particular her black, pointed stiletto heeled shoes, which she informed me she had purchased at a shop called 'The Liberated Lady' in the King's Road. 'One day', I said to myself, 'I'm going to have a pair of shoes like that.'

Yet the hard street world and the rich, 'out there' rockers and millionaires that it outwardly stood against, continued to collide in my own existence. One day Dad and I went down to see Alan Kent in Midhurst. Alan asked me if I'd help out and ride some horses down to a match at The River Grounds for him. So there was I jostling along with a herd of other grooms and nags and I took a shine to a horse that I was leading called 'Pistolo.' Prince Charles was in evidence that day, surrounded as ever by hoards of zealous snappers, which he always totally ignored. Pistolo had come down especially for him to play and I got a bit miffed when HRH said that the dear thing had gone, 'Like a stag'.

In June I went with Mum, Dad, Eric and Pattie to Lady's Day at Royal Ascot, because Dad and Eric joint owned a horse that was running called The Razor (which came last). We nonchalantly swished up to Eric's and Pattie lent me one of her hats because I didn't have one. Before we left for the races they all did a load of coke. Once at Ascot, we were accosted by Nigel Dempster looking for fodder for his gossip column. Dad and Eric bantered with him a bit and I thought it was all terribly 'famous' and exciting.

Then on the 22nd of that same month Anita and I went over to Sheryl's to see John Gale play in his new band. He spoke to me all night, but what with The Loony, Kevin and Max all on my case I felt that the long lost world of Chingford was far behind me. *'I'm stepping out, I'm moving on, I'm going to see the world..'* ('Steppin' Out': ELO) Or so I believed.

And indeed I *did* step out to see the world of the well to do once more at a Polo match in Windsor and I met up with Charlie Graham who took me out for a meal at a restaurant in the shadow of The Castle. He walked on the outside of the pavement, he ordered for me from the menu and then he said that he thought that I spoke very commonly, like Twiggy. Well, you try telling that to the footballers at Higham's Park matey 'and they won't believe you.' Then the very next night Ronnie Driver (father of actress Minnie) invited us to a Polo bash at his club in London and I had a fine old time dancing the night away with Oliver Ellis and swapping gossip with Sarah Ferguson.

I accompanied my parents to a bizarre party at a grand Georgian mansion in Essex. We took the silver Jensen and the power steering belt broke as we went through Epping. This caused a big row between Ma and Pa, ('This car is rubbish, you knew there was something wrong with it, why did you bring it?' 'Shut the fuck up you silly old bag or I am going to kill you.' Etc, etc)

And so we ended up having to get a cab to our destination. Finally, we found ourselves bowling along down a mile long drive, from which lush green pastures sloped away bounded by post and rail fencing. A final curve led up to an imposing white portico flanked with Doric columns. Once inside though, the guests appeared in the main to be completely out of their trees and I was bored to death. 'What a disappointment' I thought, as I tucked into some opiated fudge and crashed out upon a sofa. I think this party had a Chelsea connection, and that was a place where Dad often hung out.

Dad knew Terry De Havilland whose shoe shop 'Cobblers to the World' was situated in the King's Road. Terry came to dinner with us in Harrow one day and he brought Angie Bowie along with him. She was a very loud, hilariously funny individual and I really warmed to her as she kept the conversation bouncing along and laden with witticisms. Chelsea was also home to a freaky sixties boutique named 'Granny Takes a Trip', whose shop front was once famed for featuring half a car stuck through its window. A person with a poet's name, whom Number 2 and I renamed 'Gollum' (because of his highly stoned and obsequious manner), ran this establishment. What was really going on here behind the racks of expensive clothing was smack dealing on a massive scale. Local gangsters were fencing hot jewellery and other stolen goods, whilst true to nineteen-seventies cop mythology, the police were getting regular pay offs not to bust.

Meanwhile, our cars and possessions were also heading off in the same direction. The gold fob watch bought by Mum and the silver punch bowl and cups given to us by Robert Stigwood, disappeared into never to be redeemed hock. One Range Rover went off to be blown up in a film (the other had been left in Nigeria). The prop shaft on the white Jensen broke just as Dad was pulling away at some traffic lights, causing extensive damage to the underside. It remained at the Jensen workshop, in lieu of payment and we never saw it again. The silver Jensen eventually went to the crusher for the insurance. Being then car-less, Sean sold us a white, 3:0 Litre, Ford Granada GXL and one day, whilst I was still in my wellies after mucking out, Dad decided we were going straight up to Chelsea. On the way, the car started to make an ominous knocking sound. We pulled into a garage and it took a pint of oil, which Dad said was all Mum's fault. We drove on, only to be treated to, knock, knock, knock, CRASH! As the piston went through the block, spewing oil all over the windscreen, right in front of The Hoover building on the A40. We got a black cab into town to find that a skeletal dark-haired girl and a really camp bloke with long blond locks (who kept banging on about his Carmen Rollers) were manning the shop. All sorts of dodgy dealings were going on out the back, but I tried hard not to notice.

Subterfuge was rife in the personal lives of those around me. Dad brought Number 2 along with me to meet Eric and Pattie at his manager Roger Forrester's place and then afterwards he dropped me off round the corner from home to walk in separately as I was supposed to have been at Anita's. I was forever being nominated as the secret bloody postman as I carried letters from Dad to Number 2 and from Sean to Janet when she was supposed to be somebody else's girlfriend. This same spirit of deception rapidly carried over into the rest of our lives because the next thing that happened was that Basualdo and a fellow Argy got into a livery bill dispute with Dad. Basically, I think that they expected him to pay it all because they thought they were on to a good thing. So Dad decided to enlist the help of some Chelsea hard nuts who would help us nick some horses in order to settle the debt.

Down at The Water Rat pub in Chelsea's World's End, there drank some very hard, hard nuts indeed. None other than the legendary John 'I can balance five beer mugs on the end of my nob' Bindon and his crew became our drinking pals. I sat with them as they merrily recounted jolly things they had done to people, such as sticking knives up their victim's backsides and other charming pursuits. I would be there smiling away, but these people gave off such an unmistakeable air of menace that I was secretly crying out, 'Help!'

So, Bindon's crew came up to Ashton one night, and I, along with Brigitte and a gangster named Lenny, rode three horses in rugs and head collars down the pitch-black lanes as the headlights of a Jag (that was being driven slowly behind us by yet another scary heavy) illuminated our way. This incident inevitably had its repercussions. There followed a 'misunderstanding' about how much gangster work had to be done and how much it was going to cost. The result of this was that Bindon said if we didn't give him £500 he would come and kill our horses. What followed was a mad panic, in which we rushed our horses

Dad and I in Neasden, Summer 1966, in the room where Cream were formed.

Plain me and lovely Louise. Harrow, 1972.

Acapulco, Mexico, 1967.

Fancy Dress party at
Stigwood's Stanmore mansion, 1968
(spiders in ruffs out of shot).

Janet and I being 'silly' in wigs outside
'Camelot' the Harrow house, 1974.

Purple Tutu and Gold Discs.
Harrow, 1972.

The family in Harrow, 1969.

Fancy restaurant, Marbella.
Mum, Jane Gurvitz, Paul Gurvitz,
me and dad. August 1974.

Left: Sheryl and I with 'The T-Set', Isle of Wight, May, 1975.

Below: Christmas in Harrow 1976. From left; Anthony, Pamela, Mum, Dad, Grandma, Grandpa (mum's parents) & lots of polo sticks!

Horses and grooms, Tidworth 1976. Me in the centre with Chamango, Richard (left with ciggie) who saved me from the 'tent collapse'.

LINDA'S PICTURES

Hello Ginger + family — Remember the ol' days? Here's your Book. Love Linda London '76

Left: 'Rather ambiguously thought my mother!' Linda McCartney 1976.

Dad in one of the Jensen FFs, early seventies. I spent years in that passenger seat!

Left: 'Moody in the Paddock' for Annie Nightingale, 1977. Me, Leda, Judith & Dad.

Below: Doing my Gene Kelly in 'Anchors Aweigh' impression.
Woolbedding, Sussex, 1977.

My second mum and dad, Rita and Bob, with family. Sheryl gets wed at 5 months pregnant. Jubilee (formerly Trumans) Sports Ground, Highams Park, note the yellow roses. September, 1977.

International Polo, 1978. I hung out with these guys.

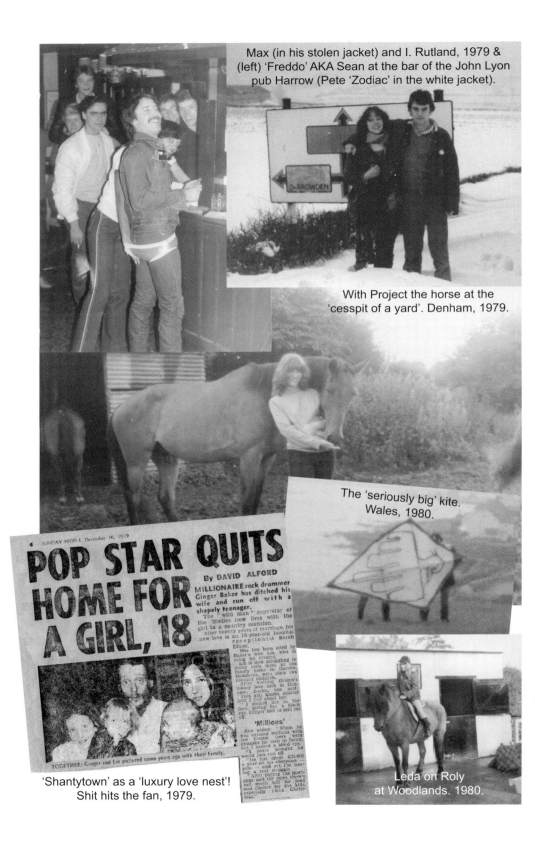

Max (in his stolen jacket) and I. Rutland, 1979 &
(left) 'Freddo' AKA Sean at the bar of the John Lyon
pub Harrow (Pete 'Zodiac' in the white jacket).

With Project the horse at the
'cesspit of a yard'. Denham, 1979.

The 'seriously big' kite.
Wales, 1980.

'Shantytown' as a 'luxury love nest'!
Shit hits the fan, 1979.

Leda on Roly
at Woodlands. 1980.

More surrogate parents. Alan and Gayle, circa 1980.

With Jayne in the Space Invader dresses. Seer Green, 1981.

Leda and I before we went 'punk', with our cousins and the 'crochet dress'. Bexley, 1981.

Me (in the 21st birthday dress) and Anita at Grandma's. West Harrow, 1981.

Solo the Wonder Dog.

Left: Lace (me) vs Spots!
Dad marries Number 2
in Italy, 1983.

Below: Leda and I, Glastonbury
Festival, 1984.

Below, left: Robert and I in the garden.
Harrow, November, 1984.

Below, right: Mum and I. The last Christmas
at the old house (we didn't know it yet).
Harrow, December, 1984.

to a secr
an

n safe. Mum went ballistic
Bindon's bundle of cash.
957 movie 'Night of the
e handed directly to the
nd ensures that within
aken away by demons.
that long after this that
ohn Darke murder at
l by all accounts was not
at I really enjoyed his
Quadrophenia'.
k became increasingly
l model, rumoured to
to keep her thin and
10 was sent out riding
k bleeding from every
is all. 'Look East', the
evening TV show
d later on we got
ere spreads in the
of Dad wielding polo

s from the Harrow
d come over to the
ht, after his darts
t
ev
1, Dad promised
drum solo when we got back to
the house. However, as he switched on the light the bulb
blew and he decided that the entertainment was off. So
much heckling followed this announcement that he said,
'Fuck it' he could play in the dark anyway and this is what
he did. People crowded into the ramshackle front room
sitting on side boards and squashed next to cupboards,
with only their fag ends illuminating the darkness and

were rendered speechless and blown away by a rendition of Mr B at his finest.

Dad had some other friends on the Rothschild estate who were involved with taking vehicles across the Sahara desert and this was another link to his being up there. This couple had a fourteen year-old son whom I got off with one night, in the back of a Land Rover on the way back from a party. I had done this at the behest of Brigitte and Number 2, who thought this would be a good ploy to get him to score us all some pot to smoke the next day when Dad was away (why couldn't we just ask him?). Nevertheless, he brought the gear round as requested and I sent the poor boy away. We (Number 2, Brigitte and I and possibly some others) were also drinking and proceeded to get completely off our faces. Consequently, they were all sick and retired to bed leaving me as the only person left standing who was capable of looking after all the horses. Ho hum.

When Number 2 failed her A' levels (I wonder why), the only alcohol that we could find to drink was gin. Dad was away again in Chelsea, so we got sloshed then gave the horses a bath and turned them out in the field for the day. Number 2 was a very competent classical pianist, and as we had a piano there I would wheedle her into to playing my favourite, which was Beethoven's 'Pathetique'. The powerful notes of this moving piece of music would float out of the open windows as Brigitte and I persuaded Max and Kieron (who were chefs) to cook us some dinner. When Dad was about we'd all eat cheese on toast and play poker for pretend money and I once won several thousand. Once or twice Mum appeared, but not when Number 2 was about obviously.

In July, we had another brief taste of the old high-life when we attended The International Polo at Windsor for the last time in a long time. I wore beige peg-top trews, a pale shirt, a cream checked waistcoat, a yellow satin jacket and clogs. Sounds awful, and it was. Janet came along in her Mini and a highly amusing and good-looking friend of Dad's named Phil Rhodes took a shine to her. As I was in tow, Phil managed to talk poor Oli Ellis into tagging along and they took us out to dinner at a Chinese restaurant after the match. We went back to 'Carvers', Phil's incredible Tudor house in Hazlemere, where we had coffee and played about with a colourful assortment of crazy canine friends. Janet drove me home and as usual she had added yet another admirer to her list, whilst I had merely added yet another one that I hadn't a hope of winning, to mine.

Autumn was soon upon us and Mr B's cash was disappearing as fast as the leaves off the sad trees that waved their branches about the eaves of the draughty farmhouse. Word came that we would be leaving soon and some of the horses had already gone. A truck arrived one day to collect the drum kit. Dad was often absent and Max and I sat alone there for several days, living off bread and soup, smoking fags and fending off the various bailiffs that kept turning up on the doorstep. Eventually, Brigitte returned from a visit home and we arranged for transport to take our remaining horses back to the Home Counties. Brig and Kieron came to stay in Harrow briefly along with Max, but he left soon after to go and work for his Dad at a pub called 'The Boot and Shoe' in South Luffenham, up in Rutland.

The potty Polebrook era was over. We wintered the horses at a run down yard in Breakspeare Road, Ruislip, called Willow Tree Farm. In the late '70's, this was a ramshackle place with decrepit old stables roofed with corrugated tin and it was owned or rented by a very fat, illiterate, Traveller type chap called Paddy Cash who tried it on with Mum and drove a blue Mercedes. A 'For Sale' notice appeared briefly outside our Harrow home and there were noisy arguments that revolved around the issue of the Gas being cut off at any moment. None of this came to pass and I think that Eric had something to do with saving the day on that particular occasion.

Then in December, Anita and I had decided to have a joint eighteenth birthday party (even though her big day had happened back in September). Her grandmother had just died and so it took place at the now empty house in Edgware. Dad and Number 2 arrived there long before anyone else did and then the front door jammed so that everyone had to troop round the back way to gain entrance. Both Max and the Loony were there, which was a tad stressful, but *'it's my party and I'll cry if I want to'* and all that. Things quite clearly were not what they once had been.

> *'Mr Blue, you did it right,*
> *But soon comes Mr Night*
> *Creeping over, now his hand is on your shoulder.*
> *Never mind, I'll remember you this way.'*
> ('Mr Blue Sky', ELO)

CHAPTER SEVEN
Our House: 1979

Once again, I found myself in the same predicament that I'd been in the previous winter, which was that I had the horses in one place and the boyfriend in another. Only this time it was the man who was to the north of Watford Gap. Consequently, I was continually up and down from Kings Cross to Peterborough courtesy of good old British Rail. In the real world, this was 'The Winter of our Discontent', with rubbish piling up in the streets and the unions going head to head with Callaghan. All I was concerned about though, was that the snow or the strikes wouldn't stop the trains from running so that I could go and see Max at 'The Boot and Shoe'. I spent a pleasant New Year up there and he and a friend called Blod (who drove about flashily in a red Triumph Stag) did 'first footing'. The two of them burst noisily into the bar out of the stormy night with snowflakes glistening in their dark hair.

Max's step mum was a glamorous blonde ex-bunny girl, called Jeanette and as his Dad was also a chef we always got well fed. Max would take me into the market town of Stamford, where we'd have Welsh Rarebit for lunch and in the evenings we'd boogie on down to songs like 'Disco Inferno' at the Riverside nightclub. On one occasion, Max met me at the station and he was wearing a beautiful blue satin jacket with a mandarin collar. 'How much was that?' I asked, 'Nothing', he replied 'I went into the shop, put it on and walked out.'

His younger brother Julian was now living with their mum in the grim industrial town of Corby, where he had found a job at the steel works. Max and I went up to see him. The place was great for shopping, because everything was dirt-cheap and we had a drink at a pub in the grey utilitarian shopping centre, where some of the large Scottish population were celebrating a wedding. Suddenly, a casual remark offended one of their party and a drunken brawl broke out, which involved women gleefully bashing their men on the heads with whatever came to hand. But the fracas died down just as quickly as it had begun and soon they were all hugging each other and in harmony once more. Meanwhile, we sat quietly drinking with looks of mild surprise upon our faces.

But although Max and I got on well enough, the distance issue began to get irksome. Before I'd left Polebrook, Max had mooted the idea of us living together but I wasn't keen. As we spent more time apart I found it did make the heart grow fonder, whereas for him I think it was the reverse. But then he was happy in his new life, whilst I on the other hand, was on the look out for any escape route possible. Neither of us was being faithful either. I was still nobbing the Loony on odd occasions in the caravan that was parked in the driveway of his parent's house on The Fairway in North Wembley and Max had started seeing a barmaid from the pub. We often sang Elton's 'Part Time Love' to each other. *'Don't tell me what to do, when you've been doing it too / because you, me and everybody got a part time love.'*

Soon enough, I got dumped and so did Mum. Just as I was enjoying my social life in Harrow again as well.

There were nights when our crowd would go to dire discos at a club called 'Tudors' opposite the Civic Centre.

Or else we'd go to a biker's pub in the town centre called 'The Gateway', where hundreds of old pennies were displayed under Perspex at the bar. The evening would often be rounded off with a visit to The Pie Stand, which was Sean's favourite place and we'd hang about there eating disgusting things swimming in ketchup and checking out the various interesting motors that cruised by.

After Donna's twenty-first birthday party in Watford, a bunch of us discovered that we were stuck in a vehicle in a car park with the barrier locked down. Brett jumped out to try and lift the thing, which then came off in his hand just as a policeman came ambling around the corner. 'Evening officer,' says Brett and we all got carted off to Watford nick.

That was the night that Sean smashed his MG into a lamppost up by the roundabout at Northwick Park. Luckily for him, the hospital was only about 100 yards away.

But all this was about to change. Somewhere along the course of his day-to-day meanderings Dad met up with a bloke named Clive. Clive was a very rich businessman, who liked to tell a story about how he had been searching for a personalised number plate and one day he saw it on some battered old wreck that was being driven by a shabby guy. Clive stopped him and offered him fifty quid for the number and the guy went off happy. But Clive was even happier because the number had really been worth thousands. That's what he was like. He lived with his family in the upmarket Buckinghamshire village of Gerrard's Cross. His house had in fact once belonged to one of the Bee Gee's and it still had its gaudy blue and silver mirror tiled bathroom in situ. More importantly as far as we were concerned, Clive also had a lovely stable yard called 'Outfields', situated at the top of Bowstridge Lane in Chalfont St Giles. One of our horses (Big Boy) found himself at livery there on another muddled 'who exactly is paying for this?' undertaking. I suppose it goes like this, 'When I sell it, I'll pay you.'

Number 2 was now hot on persuading Dad to leave home and I was for some reason convinced that we were off to Clive's pristine stables. I was more than happy to hang about there because I was trying desperately to ingratiate myself with this very hard looking girl groom who lived in a caravan on the yard with the most beautiful man that I had ever seen.

When the shit hit the proverbial, as it was bound to do eventually, all hell was let loose. My old boyfriend (and still occasional lover) The Loony had at one time had some semi-incestuous obsession with his sister (they were adopted so it wasn't quite that bad) and as a result of her saying she was leaving home to go off with us he had a bit of an attack. He was discovered late one night straddled precariously across his roof brandishing an air rifle (with which I discovered later, he had already shot his cat) and threatening to kill us all. The police came and took him away and needless to say we didn't get any sleep at our house either.

Dad quickly rented rooms for us at a large but very run down house called 'Foxgloves' in Baker's Wood (if they could), Denham. This sad and decrepit pile belonged to an old widower named Arthur. Out the back, was a paddock with a shelter and cowsheds, which could (after a fashion) be converted into stables. I referred to it disdainfully as a 'cesspit of a yard'.

Arthur shared his pad with two ancient dogs and an amusing parrot. He was quite a jovial chap to begin with and went out and about a lot in his brown Triumph

Dolomite Estate. After a while, I think he got a bit fed up with us though and from time to time concerned friends and relatives would appear to check out if we were intent on sending him to his grave prematurely and/or spending their inheritance.

The cavernous and cobwebby kitchen was home to an enormous and ancient Aga, on which a large old kettle boiled noisily most of the time. Oh, how the mighty have fallen indeed. Mum sent all our stuff along in black bin bags and I was stuck in a tiny front bedroom with only an electric bar fire for heat. It was cold so I left it on all night. The horses arrived but soon they began to disappear. Some were sold and some went to Southall Market (this usually meant 'Frenchman's Dinner'). In the end, we had three or four left including Mango. It was more than shabby in dingy Denham and I was more than heartily pissed off. So to cheer myself up I haunted the glamorous stables up at Chalfont and lusted over and daydreamed about the beautiful man who would save me from drudgery. Yes, this also seemed like a marvellously good idea.

'The Bell,' so named by my sister Leda because the outline of his mullet hairstyle resembled said object, was as I have already mentioned, breathtaking to say the least. If you have seen the 2000 film *'Almost Famous'*, he was a dead ringer for the lead guitarist called Russell in the fictional rock band 'Stillwater'. In fact, I can never watch that film without being amazed at the resemblance. His face, framed by long dark curls, boasted high cheekbones and an aquiline nose; he had piercing and unusual green eyes and a regulation seventies-style droopy moustache. He was nearly twenty-one, he wore silver earrings and he'd failed his A' levels 'cos he was on acid. How cool can you possibly be eh? Long nights in the little room at

Denham were taken up with detailed imaginings of what might happen if he decided that he liked me. Meanwhile, I managed to get friendly with his girlfriend, which in the light of her offish and brittle personality was to my mind, a great achievement. Anyway, along with Dad and Number 2 and a local blacksmith named Dell and his wife Mags, we all became drinking buddies quite soon. Then just before real life descended on me for the duration; rock star world staged its farewell performance.

On Saturday 19th May 1979, Toerag the dog, Dad, Number 2 and I attended a lavish star-studded party at Eric Clapton's Ewhurst mansion, on the occasion of his marriage to the fey and enchanting Pattie Boyd. Eric had laughed his head off whenever we had turned up to visit him in more recent times, this is because we often rattled up his driveway in the most ridiculous old bangers that you have ever seen. (One of these was an ancient silver Renault Five, the floor pan of which was composed entirely of fibreglass.) I mention this merely to highlight the huge disparity between us and the other wedding guests, because there can be no doubt that we looked more like a bunch of caravan dwellers from the site just down the road! There had been no rushing off to the shops for a new outfit to wear, because there was no money to buy such a thing. Instead, I wore a skin-tight grey cord pencil skirt I'd bought in a sale at Top Shop some considerable time before. It had a long split front and back, and the one at the back had been gradually splitting further and further under the strain of having to deal with my rather ample rear end, so I had made an attempt at repairing it with grey cotton. With my sewing skills, this meant that large untidy stitches would certainly have been on view. I had on a pair of brown snakeskin peep toe stiletto heeled sandals and dressed it all up with the old

lilac lurex tank top I'd worn at Louise's Maida Vale party
back in 1974. But nobody appeared to notice because they
probably thought, 'Oh, these famous types, they're *so*
eccentric you know.'

Once inside though, you couldn't help but notice that
the place was absolutely stuffed with more stars than you
could possibly imagine and Number 2 being a bit dense,
kept asking me to explain who they all were to her. Eric
greeted us in the kitchen. Though in his book he says he
was hiding upstairs, I definitely saw him and he said I
looked 'beautiful' so he was probably by this stage very
drunk. Not surprisingly, I was soon off my face too as the
champagne flowed freely.

Pattie looked as stunningly beautiful as ever in a tight,
mauve long sleeved top and leggings, over which she wore
a printed, sarong style silk skirt, clinched at the waist with
a wide belt and high-heeled mules. Her hair was elegantly
swept up and as usual I found her to be delightfully warm
and charming (how I longed to be her). After weaving
about the room ogling the famous faces, I found myself
speaking to Paul McCartney (whom I had been introduced
to a great many years previously at the London premier of
The Beatle's film 'Yellow Submarine'). I made some
pathetic small talk by recounting this riveting fact to him,
when Linda barged along and demanded to know, 'Well
who are you then?'

In fact, Linda had known my Dad quite well in the
'sixties, when Cream had toured the U.S. and she had built
up an extensive portfolio of photographs of many of the
decade's greatest bands. Later on, when Paul was doing
some recording for the 'Band on the Run' album at Dad's
Lagos studios, she had sent us a book of her photos
entitled, 'Linda's Pictures' and had written, 'Remember
the old days?' rather ambiguously (thought my mother) in

the flyleaf. As I meandered over to the buffet, Linda's oldest daughter Heather, who was at that time a striking looking punk with pink hair, accosted Dad with the words, 'Oh Ginger, you've made my hair stand on end!'

I noticed a very pretty little girl with long dark hair who stood quietly next to the statuesque Jerry Hall and she turned out to be Jade Jagger. Jerry was dressed in what looked like a long fuchsia pink toga and the thing that impressed me most about her, was the fact that her make-up stayed perfectly intact the whole night. She'd only just left Bryan Ferry for Mr Jagger and a buzz of a rumour reverberated through the guests that Bryan had refused to enter the place as a result. Mick was there of course, and when he was speaking to Dad and I was hovering about (to get a better look as you do), I revised my opinion of him and decided that in the flesh, yes, he was very sexy indeed.

For some inadequately explored reason, Dad then decided to ingest one of Lonnie Donnegan's heart tablets, which not surprisingly made him feel rather ill. So a bunch of kindhearted celebrities had elected to take him for several turns around the capacious gardens in order to restore him to health. McCartney came over and assured me kindly that he would, 'Be okay.' But I can't say that I was particularly concerned, because I was by that time merrily chatting up Jeff Beck until his slightly miffed girlfriend came and retrieved him. Then I got into a conversation with Ringo Starr, which involved a discussion about the ghosts in his Beverley Hills home. Eventually, he said, 'Ginger's daughter, Ginger's daughter, will you run away with me?' To which I of course replied, 'Yes!' Okay, I know he was only joking, but things were getting desperate guys and I would gladly have sold my soul to the devil or to anyone else who wanted it, in order to avoid returning to that miserable old shanty-town in Denham.

Now sometime in the nineteen-nineties, an ex-wife of quite a well-known person also documented this 'do' of Eric's in print. In her rather fanciful account she tells us that when the great personalities of the music world got up on a little stage to play together, they begged and cajoled her to get up there with them and tinkle the ivories, because they thought she was so talented. This is utter piffle. From my end of things she made a complete spectacle of herself; so much so that I could have died with embarrassment on her behalf. For an encore, she went for a long skid on a Persian rug, much to the delight of Number 2 and myself, who nearly collapsed on the floor with laughter. I won't say that I didn't make a prat of myself as well because of course I did, in fact I annoyed Eric so much that he told me to, 'Go away' and it was then that I decided I'd better make a bit of an effort to sober up! By now, they were all being deeply self-congratulatory as only stars can be and jamming away together on that over crowded platform with Ginger and Ringo vying for space on the drum kit. Ronnie Lane sang his hit 'How Come', which was pretty good, but then you can always rely on a Mod. However, whilst having a lie down somewhere on an ornate *chaise longe*, I was treated to the most indescribable caterwauling, which turned out to be Mick Jagger singing 'I Miss You' very badly out of tune at three o'clock in the morning. Not that I even possess an ounce of his talent, but it's comforting to know that we are all human after all.

If there were stars on the ground, then there were also stars more numerous and beautiful studding the firmament outside. Yet even they were rivalled by a spectacularly huge firework display. As we all 'oohed' and 'aahed', it became clear that Dad had obviously not been paying much attention to the public information films, which from the year dot have strongly advised us to 'keep pets indoors' when large incendiary devices are going off. Toerag the dog proved our social guardians correct by taking fright and running away. That just about ruined the whole thing, as the rest of the time, all the way home and for the next six days, Dad was inconsolable and so were we! It all ended happily though, because a few days later, a local policeman who had been at the party (?), spotted the dog tied up outside a gypsy caravan nearby and so, hooray, we were all reunited in 'Shantytown' at last. (The national press did an article, identifying 'Shantytown' as a 'Luxury Love Nest', which only goes to show that you mustn't believe everything that you read in the papers.)

Yes, the *'life of ease'* was over in a flash and in order to get back to some sort of fantasy life, I started reading 'The Lord of the Rings' for the second time. But fate had decided to be merciful (or not) because one day, I went swimming with The Bell and a few others and as I came out through the turnstile, I mentioned out loud to myself that the flies of my black cords were undone. 'That's not the last time they're going to do that today' came the voice of The Bell from behind me. Crikey!

That night he took me to a pub called The Three Magpies and tried to get me drunk on Southern Comfort (no need for that dear), then together we went back to 'Shantytown'. Now what on earth could someone that beautiful see in me you have to ask yourself? The Bell was an ambitious boy and I can't help but wonder if he thought that some sort of fame, money and connection might just help him on his way? I may be wrong, but hey, I thought my luck was in for once, so who cares?

What about the stern girlfriend? The Bell always said

that he thought she was beautiful and their relationship had seemed touchingly tender. Especially on an occasion when I had witnessed him tying her stock as she got ready for a show jumping competition and she was dressed only in a white shirt, underwear and socks. Who knows what he had led her to believe in private? Because he was a tricky boy. Nevertheless, for the moment it seemed that she had embarked upon a relationship of sorts with the co-owner of the yard, a middle-aged, swaggering rogue of a bloke called Bob. Naturally I didn't press for an explanation. Then one night, when we were in one caravan on the yard at Outfields and she was in another, the sound of her uncontrollable sobbing pierced the silent darkness. Oh dear, here come the Bakers again.

To get away from all the flak, my stolen boyfriend took me on a visit to Oxford to stay with one of his brothers. We drove there in his white Ford Escort Van and on the way, we had a flat tyre and the radiator blew up. This was an eerie indication of the way in which the relationship was destined to play out, with literal and metaphorical breakdowns all the way along. In Oxford, we stayed awake 'til dawn. On the way back the next evening, we sped along the M40, with the cat's eyes glowing red and turquoise in the darkness, as I chattered away sharing all my thoughts and hopes and dreams with The Bell. But I don't think that he was listening.

However, he did introduce me to all his friends. The best of these was Alex & Jayne, a newly married couple, who lived in a yellow caravan at a farm nearby. This was a riding school known as 'Widmer Stud', that was owned by Alex's parents. It was presided over by an outrageously camp show jumper named Ross, who strode about fragrantly attired in tight jods with a silk scarf knotted carelessly around his neck (maybe he'd been down The

Tower in '75). Another friend who hung out with them was a quiet bloke called Tom. He drove an old split screen Morris Minor named 'Gulliver' that had once belonged to The Bell. This vehicle had come from The Morris Minor Centre in Bath, and had been sitting neglected in a field when the lads had put a battery in it and it started. Now it was painted bright Maroon and adorned with temple bells.

Alex made a living as a mechanic then and had a car workshop next to the yard. I spent a lot of time hanging about in the cold, so I thought that I might as well learn something whilst I was at it. (Head gaskets, servo assisted brakes, rack and pinion steering, overhead cams, oh yes, I know all about these!) One day, a member of the crew named Dave, wanted to get rid of his duff old car, so a few of them decided that it would be a wheeze to cut the white Hillman Imp into four pieces with the gas welder and bury it under the indoor school. Something that is sure to confuse the archaeologists of the future.

They held a wild party in that school one night and The Bell, along with a gay mate of Ross's decided to amuse themselves by handing me a bottle of Amyl Nitrate and insisting that I, 'Sniff it hard'. Rather reluctantly I complied, with the result that my head flew off into outer space and I nearly had a heart attack. They were immensely pleased. But that taught me a valuable lesson about Poppers that I put into force when I next encountered it some four or five years later.

In August of '79, it was Dad's 40th birthday and the polo player Phil Rhodes gave him a night out up at Dingwalls in Camden Lock. I took The Bell with me and got into the atmosphere of the place. A very unusual looking couple came over to speak to Phil. The guy had shaggy hair and was dressed in black, whilst the girl really stood out with her spiky bleached blonde hair and minimalist sixties dress. I thought I'd seen them somewhere and that's because it was Dave Stewart and Annie Lennox, who were then in the band The Tourists.

In September, The Bell and I went to Cornwall for a holiday with Alex, Jayne and Tom. We stayed in a rickety cliff-top caravan and spent the days visiting tin mines and searching for semi-precious stones on the beach at St Michael's Mount. In the evenings we'd play cards by lamplight and be very silly as the wind sighed and the waves crashed rhythmically onto the beach below us. They got me into all sorts of, I suppose, hippy music. I heard The Doors properly and was mesmerised by Jim Morrison's incredible voice. Crosby, Stills, Nash & Young's 'Déjà vu' album was played a lot and I loved the track 'Four and Twenty': *'I embrace the many-coloured beast / I grow weary of the torment can there be no peace?'*

Jethro Tull was another fave, particularly the 'Aqualung' LP. We went to see them at The Hammersmith Apollo in April 1980, and again a couple of years later at The Albert Hall. Ian Anderson, a mad bastard standing on one leg playing his flute!

For a while The Bell and I stayed at 'Shantytown' in Denham, where as usual things were getting increasingly mad. Dad had two huge cases of blue and yellow pills secreted in one of the stable lofts and he had told me not to mention them to anyone. (Oh yes, 'Would you like to come riding and take pills?' or 'Look everyone, our stables are really a drugs den'.) One day, whilst I was on my own mucking out, a policeman appeared in front of me from out of nowhere. My heart began to hammer and my brain was running over what would be the correct thing to say and do should he discover the contraband. 'Calm down, calm down', he only wants to know if his wife could come over and help with the horses? Relief flooded over me. Well of course she bloody can you marvellous man. Phew! So, the policeman's wife now became very friendly with Dad and Number 2.

Dad was then given some extremely strong Nigerian grass and one day Number 2 baked it into some biscuits with the result that we all became giggling maniacs after about ten minutes. The Bell and I were in my room when the loud ringing of the doorbell urgently claimed our attention. Nobody else seemed capable of action so I went down in my dressing gown, only to be confronted by Mr Policeman again asking for his wife. I went up and opened the door to Dad's room and saw Dad lying on the bed naked except for a mirrored waistcoat, with a pink ribbon tied around his willy and Number 2 and the policeman's wife sitting either side of him.

Yet another strange incident occurred one stormy night when we had heard loud screams coming from outside in the early hours of the morning. The daylight revealed that several shop dummies had been dismembered and placed strategically about the street. Red paint had been daubed upon the hacked off limbs and at the top of the road an old bathtub was found to be full of them. Outside our place a single hand stuck up out of the verge with most of its fingers severed. Dad thought that might have some significance to him being a drummer. There was some vague rumour that it was the anniversary of a gruesome murder that had been committed there, but I am still none the wiser. Weird or what?

Meanwhile, I was getting paid a small amount for doing the nags but most of the money was coming from the exertions of Number 2. She was working as a hospital receptionist and it's to be expected that she wasn't that keen on paying my wages and she wasn't all that keen either on any influence I might have had over Dad. We were often falling out in a spectacular fashion. I once destroyed some biscuits she had baked and she retaliated by beating me with a Wellington boot. She then told me that I had to go because they just couldn't afford me and that was fair enough. So I went to work part time at Outfields with The Bell and I took Mango the horse with me.

I also got a job working as a check out girl in a glorified supermarket in Chalfont St Giles. I had quite a laugh there with a girl named Carol and a barmy warehouse guy whom we re-named 'Ivy Clivy'. He was a member of an obscure religious sect known as the Christadelphians, so he was quite innocent and we teased him unmercifully. On one memorable occasion we had a special offer of baked beans coincidentally followed by one of toilet rolls. Well we thought it was funny. I worked the checkouts, checked in pallets of goods and was in charge of the tinned fruit aisle. I would go out at lunchtimes wearing tight pencil skirts and sit on the green outside The Merlin's Cave pub. It was okay there until some thick Irish woman accused me of stealing a pair of tights, which was just not my style (stealing that is, not the tights, they were nice but I did pay for them).

The Bell and I embarked upon a rural horsey life, proving that the ethos of Flambards was not forgotten. We set up home on the yard at Outfields in a lovely caravan complete with bathroom and a Stubbs print on the bedroom wall. The old girlfriend had left her Jilly Cooper novels and her dog behind. He was a beautiful German Shepherd cross, called Solo, but she had now gone off to live with a guy who ran a large stables in Arkley, Barnet. This bloke also owned thirteen

Dobermans whom Solo fought with, so she asked us to take care of him for her. Solo got into another fight whilst he was with us, so we paid all his vet bills and after a few months had gone by, he began to think that he was my dog. Eventually, she came along wanting him back. It did seem that he had forgotten her by then, so we said, 'No' and he then officially did become mine up until his death in 1991. So I got her man and her dog.

There were in total, thirteen dogs living out on the yard, as well as a ram named Joey, a black cat and several chickens which tended to lay whilst sitting on gates, resulting in smashed eggs everywhere. Once I arrived, thirteen dogs were sleeping in the little caravan with us. It got a bit untidy in there, so The Bell suggested that I might try doing a bit of housework. I can't say that the idea had ever occurred to me before, but I was willing to give it a go and I quite enjoyed my first stint of recipes and domestication and attempting to be normal, it was very novel. At Christmas, we had a little tree in the window and I would thrill to see its lights twinkling in a homely way as we approached it from the road.

> *'Our house is a very, very, very fine house*
> *With two cats in the yard*
> *Life used to be so hard*
> *Now everything is easy, 'cos of you.'*
> ('Our House': CSN&Y)

CHAPTER EIGHT
Blue Condition: 1980

'Don't take the wrong direction passing through..'
('Blue Condition': Cream)

T he Bell and I were destined to be together for quite
some time to come. We never really got on with
each other and I guess it was mainly his exceptional
beauty that kept me hanging on in there for so long. He
did a lot for my aesthetic sense if nothing else. We went off
to a party once when he was wearing a frogged military
jacket that my Dad had picked up in Carnaby Street in the
swinging sixties. The car we were in had a puncture just
for a change and as he laboured by the roadside changing
the wheel, I felt well pleased with myself that I had
managed to pull such a looker.

His family however, were a bit strange, although I
suppose I can talk. Upwardly mobile middle class, they
had for some years lived practically next door to Eric in
the neighbouring Surrey village of Peasmarsh. But then
The Bell's parents, younger brother and a cute little dog,
named Topsy, moved up to Flask Walk in Hampstead.
This was a fabulous place and I could never understand
why they later moved away from such a perfect location,
situated as it was, right next to the Heath, with The Flask
pub at the top of the road. Their tall Georgian house stood
directly opposite that of the actor Robert Powell and his
'Pan's People' dancer wife Babs and you could see right

into their living room. In addition to this, respected thespians such as Peter Barkworth and Pauline Collins could also be spotted in local shops and wandering about the streets.

Mother and Father Bell certainly did not approve of me. They were obsessively keen that young people should be free and have no responsibilities, which I believe was in fact code for, 'Son, please don't take up with unsuitable young ladies.' They constantly tried to find jobs for The Bell in places like Outer Mongolia, or The Hebrides, where he would be safely far away from me. Moreover, they openly expressed their belief that as my father was a drug addict and my mother was a neurotic it was inevitable that I would turn out to be the same. In fact, none of them were particularly enamoured of me, because I was so obviously lacking in culture and learning.

The Middle brother was an artist who thought that he was very good. He once took me round a gallery of Modern Art, where he gravely and very patiently explained to me the deep significance of a moody work that featured brown paper with bits of string glued meaningfully upon it. I still can't help wondering if the artist, on running out of ideas, had simply stuck the wrappings from a parcel he'd received into a frame in a fit of pique and been done with it? This arty brother had a girlfriend, also a dab hand with a brush, who was far and away more talented than him and after getting a well-deserved first for her Fine Art degree, she was awarded a coveted place at the Royal Academy. However, true to Bell family tradition, this arty brother messed her around so much that she attempted suicide, but eventually she went on to marry him and I can only wish her good luck with that.

The Bell's older sister was married to a man who was

doing a Phd at Oxford and as you may imagine everyone was terribly impressed with that. One day, we were in The John Lyon pub with her and I went up to the bar. As I stood with my back to them, innocently ordering a triple Bacardi and Coke, this sister allegedly piped up, 'Isn't it a shame that Nettie has to wear such high heels'? Yes isn't it?

The youngest boy was quite sweet. He attended the exclusive school of Beadales, and wore a yellow leather jacket. Anyway, what very odd people those Bells were.

Then my horse died in unpleasant circumstances (even now I can't talk about it, but the Bell was involved) and things started to get a bit on the dodgy side with the rich businessmen bosses at Outfields Stables. Their astounding arrogance coupled with ignorance, inevitably resulted in several cases of animal cruelty. I hold to the opinion that they would have been better off by far taking up an interest in trials bikes. That way when the wheel drops off 'cos you've hammered it through the mud, you can easily replace it. They bought horses willy nilly, from unscrupulous dealers throughout the county without having them vetted and cared not one jot when things went pear shaped. Feelings began to run high and I was very sad to have to quit our little house on the prairie. But I'm pleased to report that The Bell nicked some bits and pieces from the place and some money out of a wallet just before we scarpered.

The Bell had already bought an old, dark red Austin Cambridge Estate from Dell the blacksmith for £10 and we consequently spent a lot of time at Alex's workshop welding new sills on. I loved that car. We made curtains for the back windows (I say 'we' but in fact I didn't have anything to do with it) and took it on holiday to Wales, along with Alex, Jayne, Tom and Alex's brother Dee. Dee was like a wizard with his long blond hair and flowing beard, in fact he looked like he'd walked straight out of Carol King's song 'Tapestry'. He also had a little blond son named Jimmy, whom his wife had left him in custody of and he often had him along with him. In Wales, The Bell and I slept in the car and got soaked because it rained the whole time and the tailgate was rusty. This was in the days of the CB radio craze and we amused ourselves and terrified other drivers by going in convoy and telling each other when it was safe to overtake on blind corners. We visited the slate mines and The Museum for Alternative Technology where we bought CND badges and The Bell told me not to look at the camera, because he said he didn't want my face in any of the photos.

One day, The Bell, Dee, Tom and Alex decided to construct a giant kite. It was made from the flysheet of an old tent, with a bamboo frame and it measured a 'seriously big' 3m x 2m. The outline of a sinister looking bird of prey with wings out stretched, was daubed over it in black paint. Dee remembers that, "We had to weight it down with heavy rocks to keep it stable and we bought the local shop out of all their nylon cord. It flew fiercely and well in the strong Atlantic winds that cut across the headlands. So well in fact, that it soon wrenched free of its moorings (or the hands of whoever was attempting to hold it). Consequently, a massive kite with about ten kilos of rubble tied under it and trailing vast amounts of nylon cord was soon disappearing into the distance towards the sea. Luckily it flew, or it would've taken someone out had it hit them, their car, a cow, ten sheep or whatever. It sailed off to land almost out of sight in the water and vanished into the murky depths. A stunned silence prevailed. Then I expect someone said. 'Wow man, amazing, lets roll a joint'."

The Bell and I went on holiday yet again with Alex and Jayne and our four dogs, Pippa, Solo, Gemma and Bert. This time The Bell had bought a dark red Austin Maxi and due to the demanding terrain of roads like Hardknot Pass, the famous 'hydro-elastic' (or 'hydro-spastic') suspension collapsed. We had to prevail upon Dee to come up with a Volvo and car trailer to save us and he and Jimmy came and camped with us again for a couple of days. We were always at the end of the campsites but you could still smell the dope wafting around in the evening air and because the toilets were miles away I never dared to drink anything after about six o'clock in the evening. The showers were always grim as well and Jayne often had to protect me from the Daddy Long Legs of which I was then pathologically afraid. I have to say that I am not a girl who is cut out for camping.

We usually had a two-man tent and Alex and Jayne sometimes brought a caravan. The lads once spent about a hundred years trying to work out how to put the awning up, probably because they were a little stoned. We flew kites on the beach at Seascale where the skyline was dominated by the ominous looking cooling towers of the infamous nuclear power station. The journey back from the lakes was fairly eventful because the trailer had two punctures and we ended up stuck in glorious Wigan for a while attempting to get it fixed. Then The Bell had a go at me for getting in a strop for being tired and hungry (he said he thought I should be more caring about Jimmy and less interested in myself). It ended up taking us thirteen hours to get back down to Buckinghamshire and Jayne's silver Honda Civic clocked up fifty-two miles to the gallon because she'd had to drive so slowly.

On yet another excursion, The Bell and I went down to Falmouth in a white Ford Escort van to see the arty brother and his girlfriend. The Bell had an odd driving style, which involved him going very slow along the straight and yet ridiculously fast around the corners. We were overloaded to say the least, with two roof racks up and the heavy toolbox right behind them. On the A30 between Okehampton and Tavistock, he took a bend way too fast and lost it. We just missed a big old Saab going in the opposite direction, but then an orange Hillman Imp full of old grannies hit us broadsides and we slammed into the black and white chevron marking the corner. The impact sent the two roof racks crashing on to the bonnet and I banged my head. 'Are you okay?' asked The Bell. I was. He had a bag of grass and pills in the glove compartment, which he promptly threw behind the chevron for safekeeping before the emergency services arrived in force and happily informed me that they usually had to cut bodies out of the wreckage at that particular accident black spot. The van incidentally, was a write off (or my side was anyway, see Billy Bragg!).

Alex and Jayne were already in Cornwall and we had previously arranged to meet them in a designated pub. Alex was calmly sipping his pint when the strange barman, holding a telephone receiver aloft, shouted over, 'Are you Alex?' 'Yes', came his rather wary reply. 'Well, your friend has just crashed his car and is on the phone here asking for you to come and pick him up.' '#****#!' said Alex.

So the two of them drove back up to collect us from a hotel in Tavistock where I was sat having a large drink and my first cigarette for a year. On the way back past the chevrons we stopped to pick up the stash, but it had mysteriously disappeared! What the explanation for that is I just don't know.

On another trip that The Bell and I went on, we had a

puncture again but the spare was flat. So he left me in the vehicle talking to some cows in a field by the side of the road whilst he hitched a lift to go and get the tyre inflated. As luck would have it, he got picked up by, in his words, 'Some freaks on a trip to the seaside.' And arrived back not only with the tyre repaired, but also well out of it.

Back in Bucks, we all went to Beccy Fair, The Bell won me a mirror at a shooting game, I had my photo taken with some scary monkeys dressed in cardigans and a mate called Jez and I got the giggles in the car on the way back. The Bell and I were now living at Mum's for a spell and I was secretly and unwisely taking my younger siblings over to Denham on odd occasions to see Dad because Mum would not allow it. But of course Mum found out, with the predictable result that she then tried to kill everyone. She stormed over to Denham and I locked myself in the toilet. Then she attacked Number 2 and Dad broke her ribs whilst prizing her off. I did phone the police for assistance, but in those days the only response you got was, 'We don't deal with domestics.'

Next thing we knew, Dad had stolen the kids and taken them off to his mother and sister in Bexley and then Mum got an injunction and retrieved them. The exact same thing had happened ten years previously, only then with me involved as well. My poor siblings did not enjoy this period in time very much. Eventually, we all had to go up to the Law Courts in The Strand, where they had a big and heavy Mum vs Dad battle with nearly everyone on Dad's side. After that, Mum didn't speak to me for three years. I went back to do Dad's horses in Denham again and commuted by train from my grandparent's house, where I was now staying, in West Harrow. Where The Bell went to during that time I have no idea, off being ambitious somewhere no doubt.

When Dad and Number 2 had first moved to Denham, it was ostensibly to get away from drugs. However, not long after their arrival, Dad had decided to pop down to the local farm to buy some eggs. Immediately he entered the place, the scruffy long-haired thirty-something son of the proprietor appeared and said, 'Hello Ginger, fancy a toot?' Now this is junkie parlance for, 'Good afternoon, would you care to partake of a snort of heroin?' Unbeknownst to us, we had in fact settled in the midst of a veritable hive of smack heads. Major big league dealers were at that time operating out of West Drayton and can congratulate themselves on being at least indirectly responsible for the death from AIDS of many of the people whom I met at that time, including the aforementioned son of the market trader.

Winter arrived and Dad got some work driving the market bloke's truck to the Western International Market in the early mornings. On the way back he would pick me up from Uxbridge tube station. One December morning, I climbed up into the cab and the radio was on. 'John Lennon's just been shot dead' said Dad.

We would all sit round the wooden table in the window bay of the front room at 'Shantytown'/Denham and Number 2 would cook us a hearty breakfast. One morning, we had an extra and very lively person round to share our eggs on toast. Dad had managed to get some more work helping this brickie / master builder bloke that he had met through the local drug scene. His name was Dave, he was twenty-nine and he was very dark and swarthy and acted well cocky. He had black curls, brown eyes, big smile, big nose and a fine pair of thighs encased in black jeans. I didn't like him. In fact, I didn't like him for about two days and then I decided that I was madly in love with him. Not that I approved of the drug thing, but he and two of his brothers were the sort of people whose charm was so great that they lit the room. They were The Carps, (Carpenters) and there were loads of them, but Dave, Tony and Jimmy were really something special in my book. It was a shame that they never thought the same about me.

Now in December, The Bell had gone off down to Newlyn, in Cornwall to decorate a cottage for some friends of his parents (nice try Bells), so he was off the scene. Because I was really smitten, Dave took me out for a drink once or twice, even though he was married / separated, with two kids. However, the uncertainty of a druggie who was so much older and so fly, made me hesitate. At the same time, Number 2 informed me that he had also taken *her* out and told her he was madly in love with her and I have no cause to doubt it. In fact, it was Dad that he really cared about in a male bonding sort of a way.

The next thing that happened, was that The Bell said I could go down to Cornwall for my birthday, so off I went, planning to end it with him and run off with Dave when I got back. For some reason, The Bell got *very* excited at the thought of me being interested in somebody else. But I (mis)interpreted this to mean that he still cared for me and did not wish to end it. I spent the day of my twentieth birthday watching huge waves crash spectacularly over The Lizard at Land's End and in the evening we went for a drink in a little pub in Newlyn. When I returned I still loved Dave, but I wasn't going to go for it and he didn't press it.

Dave was living in a shared house in Churchfield Lane at Chalfont St Peter. He would soon be moving out, but he said that there was a spare bed-sit there on the top floor and that I could have it for £12 per week. So I moved in there and The Bell bought me a Cheese Plant. On my first tentative night in my own place, Dave invited me down to his bare room. How exciting! He had a cup of coffee and made me a tea. We sat together on his settee watching the telly, which was showing a music programme with Hazel O'Connor on it. She was the big thing then and I loved the film 'Breaking Glass' with Phil Daniels in it, sigh. So, there was Hazel and she started to sing, *'You drink your coffee and I sip my tea / and we're sitting here playing so cool thinking what will be will be..'*

Chills ran down my spine as I began to wonder if she could actually see me (yes, I know there is a medical term for this). However after some little time had passed, Dave unfortunately really did *'...just politely, say goodnight.'* Shit!

But we continued to play about, probably because I wanted it. He took me shopping and bought me some trousers. He was always such fantastic company and made me feel alive. On New Years Eve, there was a big party at my new place and as midnight struck, Dave and I were kissing at the bottom of the stairs, whilst The Bell, who had retired early with a lame excuse, slept up in my room.

CHAPTER NINE
Buckinghamshire Babylon: 1981

I had some good times at that flat in Churchfield Lane. The Bell lived there with me intermittently depending on whether he thought I was chucked or not. In the meantime, I made some more friends. The first floor front room over looked Chalfont St Peter High Street and was home to a couple named Alan and Gayle. He was a longhaired hippy who worked in a furniture shop and he had a strangely amusing brother with even longer hair, called Brian. Gayle, who was a lot younger than Alan (and a year younger than me), was a quiet, kind hearted, petite and beautiful girl with a strong sense of self. When they had first met dad at their previous address, he had walked straight over their bed, which at that time was just a mattress on the floor. Gayle was furious and said to Alan, 'That bloody man just walked straight over our bed with his boots on!' And Alan said, 'But that's Ginger Baker', 'I don't care who it bloody is, he's not walking over my bed!' came Gayle's spirited reply.

These two looked after me a lot and were like surrogate parents. I needed to work and Alan found an advert for a groom in the local paper. By some quirk of fate I actually managed to land the job. This entailed looking after six horses for five and a half days a week, at a stable yard called 'Woodlands', up on Narcot Lane. The wages were £35 per week and I was up on my own two feet at last. Woodlands Farm was in walking distance of Churchfield

Lane. It was set well back from the road and had a long driveway, which led up to the yard and a bungalow surrounded by paddocks. It belonged to a bloke called Geoff whose wife had left him for someone else and he had remained there with his two horse-riding children.

These were a teenage girl and her younger brother who were in turn cared for by their grandparents; a great couple that Leda and I soon came to know as, 'Nannie' and 'Freddums'. Geoff drove a dark green V reg, Ford Capri Ghia, he was thirty-six years old, had dark hair and he wore thick, black framed glasses and string vests, which became the cause of much hilarity. So much so in fact, that Nannie and I would often be helpless with laughter at the sight of these vests going round in the washing machine. The four-legged occupants of the farm were show ponies and the children competed in working hunter classes and one-day events. I would often walk to work at 5:am in order to get everything ready for a show and my organisational skills were such that they soon nicknamed me 'Adolf.' Nevertheless, I did get an extra tenner if we won, which happened quite often. Sometimes, we'd stop off at the grand house of an acquaintance of theirs and being the groom I wasn't allowed in and had to sit out on the terrace.

My sister Leda was now thirteen and I got her a job at the weekends helping me out. She would get the train over and stay with me on Friday and Saturday nights and on school holidays. Sometimes she would be over at Dads doing his lot as well and one day she decided to ride Piggy over to mine, park him up, help me out and then go back. However, along the way she met up with some other horse riders whom I knew and Pig got a bit over excited. This involved him getting very strong and running into a barbed wire fence, which he had spotted quite a while before Leda did. So Pig stopped hard and Leda was deposited in the wire. By the time she arrived at Woodlands she looked a right state. Her blue anorak was ripped and torn from the wire. Piggy was covered in a white foam of sweat and because he threw his head about so much, he'd snapped his standing martingale (designed to control just this habit), which was flapping up and down. She then came out for a normal ride with me on a different horse and I repaired her and sent her back.

We had a horse at Woodlands who got a bit lairy sometimes as well and he was a big fat, strawberry roan coloured cob named Roly (show name: Sugar Puff). He had allegedly been the horse that International rider Jane Kidd (sister of polo playing/ex show jumper Johnny, father of, etc) had bought to get herself back in the saddle after she broke her back. I don't know if this is true. Occasionally, Roly would get very strong and piss off. As we found out one day when Leda was cantering along in front of me, suddenly she turned round and said, 'Bye Nettie', before disappearing at great speed in a cloud of dust.

When Leda came over at the weekends, Alan and Gayle would let her sit in with them if I was out at the pub. Dope smoking was rife amongst us all and I'd come back to find her with her long ginger hair wildly crimped, wearing black eyeliner and stoned out of her box! Then I'd have a smoke but I couldn't handle strong stuff like Morrocan, so they'd often pretend it was something else to stitch me up. Once I nearly passed out in The Baker's Arms after some particularly strong Double O Zero.

One day, we were all out of it in A&G'S room, when someone knocked on the door. Alan answered, and this person, whom we knew, informed him in an agitated manner that they'd just seen a policeman walking about outside. There then followed a mad panic in which everyone ran about like headless chickens tidying up and hiding the evidence. The Bell threw his stash out of the window directly onto the shopping street below. Of course, it was a false alarm and was merely a policeman moving in to the place next door. It was very amusing to watch The Bell mingling nonchalantly with the busy shoppers as he successfully retrieved his gear.

Upstairs in the room next to mine, lived a guy called Derek who had a mate also named Derek. I couldn't roll a joint at that time, so if I had any gear I would often pop into Derek's and get him to roll one for me. One day, I was sitting in my room, the two Derek's were playing Eric Clapton's 'Wonderful Tonight' on their guitars next door and I thought I would pop in and get them to roll me a 'dodat' as we all liked to call 'joints' in those days. Unfortunately, I had left my keys in my door and all of a sudden it burst open with a violent crash. Two Bodie and Doyle look-alikes straight out of the TV show The Professionals rushed into the room shouting, 'Drug squad! It's a raid!' Blimey!

I got dragged in next door until they ascertained that it was nothing to do with me. Then the Martin Shaw bloke came into my room and asked me,

'Have you ever been in trouble with the police?'

'No.'

'Oh, you're a good girl are you?'

'You can tell can't you?

He began to search my room. I looked out of the window and my heart began to beat very fast as I imagined what my grandparents would think of headlines like, **'Fallen Rock Star's Daughter Caught in Sleazy Bed-Sit Drug Bust.'** He went to my jewellery box and began to open the drawers. I was thinking, 'Oh no, that's where it is, any minute now I'm for it', but he didn't say anything. The room was in such a terrible untidy mess (as though a clothes bomb had exploded in there) that he just sighed, said, 'Stay there' and went back next-door.

I was very confused and got up to look in the jewellery box. It wasn't in there. I racked my brains in desperation, wondering what the hell I'd done with it. Finally I remembered that I had come in well out of it the previous night and put the rolled up polythene bag of grass on top of the electric fire, where it had gently unrolled itself and fallen down the back. I quickly retrieved it and stuffed the bag under the carpet. This was one time that being untidy saved my bacon.

The postscript to this particular incident was that I phoned Dad and told him to hurry over without saying why (phone might be bugged). For some reason, he apparently jumped to the conclusion that someone had given me heroin and he was going to kill them. But no, I just wanted him to take my grass. I don't mind doing these things, but in my book it's just not worth the hassle of getting caught. Along with Number 2 we went off for a drink. Later on they dropped me back at the flat but I couldn't get in at street level. This is because Alan, who hadn't been involved and was fast asleep at the time of the raid, had had heart failure and barricaded the door with tables, chairs and God knows what in case they should return. Talk about 'shutting the stable door after the horse has bolted'! This then brought an ironic slant to our nightly pursuit of playing the brilliant board game, 'It's a Raid.'

Later in the year, Leda and I went to Tony Carp's firework party where we ate some dope cake. Leda was having a marvellous time but I went into one and was hallucinating like mad. On the walk home I thought I was in another dimension and couldn't even see the pavement. Then when we went to bed I was convinced that I was going to die. I reiterated this fact loudly and my little sister had to calm me down by saying, 'It's alright man; you are *not* going to die.' I haven't eaten it since!

The actual state of the place in Churchfield Lane was pretty grim and it appeared to be owned by a geezer who ran the electrical supply shop underneath. Obviously, he wasn't that keen on making it too cosy for us lot of reprobates and it was in a shocking state of disrepair. The window frame on the landing was rotten and one day it fell off onto the path below nearly hitting some poor bugger on the head. Most of the house suffered from the damp a great deal and the walls were often covered in black mould. I painted my room about three times whilst I was there but it always came back. The bathroom in particular was pretty bad for black walls, and much to my surprise, it also had a boiler with a meter, in which you had to insert 50p to get a measured amount of hot water out. This was a new concept to me, because I had never yet encountered such a thing in my previously sheltered existence.

Alan loved his bath though and would happily sing away in there wearing a fetching pink bath hat, whilst employing his loofah as a microphone. One day, when he was gaily serenading himself, Dad arrived at the entrance door below and in response to the wonderful sounds that came floating out into the air, he picked up an old corn-on-the-cob out of the dustbin and lobbed it up into the open bathroom window much to Alan's surprise. Leda did something silly in that bathroom that involved her climbing up onto the window ledge; with the result that she accidentally knocked one of the guy's razors into the toilet. I told her to flush the chain then fish it out, as this had worked for me on another occasion with some keys. We flushed. The razor disappeared. We kept quiet. A few days later Alan said, 'The toilet's blocked up, but I can't understand why.'

In the dingy, narrow hallway at the top of the first flight of stairs was the typical bed-sit payphone and as it was right outside Alan and Gayle's door, this meant that Alan nearly always took the messages. One day, he came to me looking most irate and saying that he'd had some idiot on asking for me and claiming to be the chocolate bar character of Freddo Frog. This turned out to be Sean taking the piss as usual in a way that none of his victims found to be in the slightest bit amusing. The kitchen was pretty spare too and I mainly cooked myself spaghetti with tomato sauce and grated cheese unless Gayle fed me or I had Dad and Number 2 or Alex and Jayne round to dinner. One time, I couldn't get in the kitchen and was most annoyed to discover later that Derek and a guy named Zac had totally ruined one of my teaspoons by cooking up their smack in it.

I did my food shopping in Bishop's supermarket over the road and once Anita and I made a spectacle of ourselves when we saw Jimmy Carp down one of the aisles. We hid from him giggling and swooning in a most pathetically childish way. Another domestic chore involved Number 2, who would come over on a Tuesday night and we'd have the great excitement of going to the launderette, where we were amazed on more than one occasion to see the real Lewis Collins from 'The Professionals', lurking about outside.

I would often meet up with Gayle after work and we'd go to the White Hart and thrash young blokes at Pool, which pissed them right off. Or sometimes we'd go to The Greyhound pub down by the roundabout, where none other than Brian Connolly, lead singer from 'Sweet,' would sit on a tall stool at the bar, his blond hair still in its Glam Rock style, and drink for hours on end. This one time fantasy of a million teenage girls now looked like a man out of time and to us it appeared as if his glory days were over. If Dad came in, he would go over to Brian and they'd have a drink together, but I don't know what they talked about.

Other pubs in the area that we frequented were 'The French Horn' and 'The Jolly Farmer.' The Bell would take me to eat the best Ploughman's ever up at 'The Royal Standard of England' in Beaconsfield with Alex and Jayne. This pub also served various locally made wines of every description. Jayne and I would go out in matching knitted dresses with phallic looking space invaders emblazoned on the front and I had a pair of white stiletto baggy boots with fringing around the top. There was a wine bar in Amersham and in fact there were wine bars all over the shop in those days. One night, I had a lot of fun in there and ended up dancing upon the table, which is a past time that I have always enjoyed. The poor Bell was so mortified at the spectacle of me having a nice time, that he ignored me for three days afterwards.

Then Dad took us out *en famile* one night. He was driving a pale lilac Daimler Sovereign that he'd borrowed off Son of Market Man and we went for a meal at a restaurant called Barnard's Lodge on the A40 at West Ruislip, opposite The Master Brewer Hotel. During the meal, Dad stood up, announced that he was off to retrieve an unspecified item from the car and disappeared into the dark. When he returned, he was pushing a Supermarket trolley that contained Number 2's Jack Russell dog and when questioned by the rather harassed looking waiter he explained that in fact he had, 'Just been doing the shopping.'

He would often get pulled over by the Old Bill whilst driving home from the pub. 'Good evening Mr Baker,' the police would say as they produced the bag with the crystals in. Mr Baker always reckoned that he beat the breathalyser by inhaling clean air through his nose and out of his mouth.

In May '81, after a brief courtship, my friend Janet married Paul Barry, a dashing fellow who worked in her father's firm and along with Ethel the Aardvark they began a life financed by plenty of Quantity Surveying. When I had mentioned to The Bell that they had named the day after so short a dalliance he said, 'Well you always know when it's the right one.' There's no answer to that really is there?

Janet and Paul got married at Roxeth church on the slopes of Harrow Hill. I was a bridesmaid and a very ugly one indeed with my Lesley Judd hairstyle and snaggly goofy teeth. In hindsight I feel very sorry for the poor, beautiful Bell on being stuck with me. However, I caught the bouquet (in a 'skilful way'), much to his horror and everyone else's amusement. Whilst I was looking for a man who would be glad to pay for the pleasure of my marvellous company, I feel sure that The Bell was looking for exactly the same in a woman. He definitely did not want a useless clinger and he often told me so.

My mother was at the wedding and I was glad that although she ignored me and told a fellow guest she thought I was a 'flash bitch', she didn't try to kill me. Not long afterwards of course, it was the turn of Charles and Di to trip up the aisle. Everybody in the world got a day off except for me, who spent the afternoon creosoting a fence up at Woodlands. Dad took a break from helping Dave to build some of the new houses that were going up in Gerrard's Cross.

Dad also did some work with the bands Atomic Rooster and Hawkwind; so occasionally I would encounter the likes of Dave Brock and his ilk over at 'Shantytown.' Dad also formed another band that he took to play at Glastonbury Festival in 1981. I went along with The Bell and we met up with Dave Carp whilst we were putting up our tent (yes, I still liked him). Dad had asked us to come up to the Pyramid stage to find him, which we did, but we were impeded in our progress by an officious security Jobsworth, who got narky and refused to let me up the stairs. Luckily Dad saw me, called me to come up and the Jobsworth was really creepy after that. Are back stage areas constantly full of folks so desperate to be there that they pretend to be members of certain musician's families when they're not? The answer to this seems inexplicably to be 'yes'.

Anyway, the gig got underway and a musician called Roy Harper was on stage before Dad. The various bands all had their allotted run time due to the fact that the power had to be turned off at a designated hour in order I presume, to appease the locals. Mr Harper was obviously enjoying himself because he went on a bit long, causing Dad who was in the wings to shout, 'Hurry the fuck up' to him. This caused Mr H to get annoyed in turn and he began to incite the crowd to get angry along with him. Consequently, when Dad finally managed to get on stage, the inebriated audience were all pretty rowdy and some nutter threw a rock, which hit Dad in the face. He stopped playing and came to the microphone covered in claret. 'You've had your blood. Now can we continue?' He said.

The next day, The Bell and I sat in Michael Eavis's farmhouse kitchen whilst Dad had a good complain to him about Mr Harper and the previous night's proceedings. But I was impressed by Glastonbury. I'd never seen anything like it, even though I had already been to a few open-air gigs. In those days it resembled a medieval town and you half expected Robin Hood and his merry men to be passing through at any minute. I carried this dope smoker's pipe dream of a different life with me back to Buckinghamshire, where in August Alex and Jayne announced that they were expecting a baby. There they were getting on with life and here was The Bell, dithering as always and trying largely unsuccessfully, to further his ambitions.

Back in the land of shit shovelling, I was looking after two horses for a woman who turned out to be none other than the famous (in the horse world) Mary Robbins. In fact, I was completely unaware until several years later, that she is in fact a highly respected British Dressage judge. By sheer good luck I had Mary to teach me how to ride a horse English style, as opposed to a polo style, which is like the cowboys. The Bell had already gone down the dressage route and he and another friend Rupert, started to go and ride up at a place called Park Farm in Northwood, Middlesex, not far from Harrow. This place is now a health farm and housing development as usual, but in the days when landowners were slightly less greedy and you had some diversity in Greater London, it was a splendid equestrian establishment that trained instructors and clients alike to a decent standard and held shows in which famous names competed. I would go up there for a drink in the bar afterwards and hang out with all the working pupils who were training for their Assistant Instructor's exam. I thought that these girls looked fabulous because they all had coloured hair and loads of ear piercings from which they hung tons of sparkly, dangly earrings.

One of these girls held a fancy dress birthday party somewhere in the vicinity and I went attired as a Highwaywoman, with trousers tucked into the fringed stiletto boots (now dyed brown), a white frilled shirt and a tricorn hat with a feather. It was a pale summer evening, so we stood outside the hall for a while in the car park and

I spoke to one of the two Sarah's that The Bell was now working with at another yard nearby. Sarah had come dressed as herself and she was I suppose, the first real Goth that I ever encountered. She looked extremely striking with her waist length black hair, Cleopatra eyes, scarlet lips and that same style of wicked black stilettos as worn by the punk girl from Chelsea. I began to strongly aspire to that look. I was far more impressed with how these people looked, than I was with their boring talk about equine collection and impulsion from behind! Anyway, back at Woodlands where I worked, we had the great Mary without realising her importance and Leda and I would sing, 'Mary, makes tea bags makes tea' to the Tetley Tea tune as we cleaned the tack.

At the beginning of December '81, several tons of snow were deposited upon us from above. Leda arrived at the flat hours late that first weekend, having walked all the way there from Little Chalfont station, which was quite some distance. One day, as I was toiling away trying to get my wheelbarrow up and down the frozen ruts, my dog Solo appeared out of the blizzard like a Saint Bernard with a note tied around his neck. It was from Nannie up at the house and it read, 'Nettie, come in for your lunch.'

Outside the flat in Churchfield Lane, we all mucked about having snowball fights and Solo got so over excited that he bit a guy on the leg. This was the bloke who had gone into Dave's old room and for a while I decided I fancied him until he indicated that he liked me too and then I back-pedalled at a rate of knots. One night coming back from Seer Green, The Bell and I came across a body lying in the middle of the snowy road. Some poor drunk had been walking home along the country lane and been hit twice by drivers going in opposite directions. The Bell got out, covered him up with a dog blanket and called an ambulance.

Dad had by this time taken up again with the terrible Roy, of getaway car driving fame and they had set up Acorn recording studios in Warple Way, Acton, North West London. My twenty-first birthday was now fast approaching and so I decided to hold my party there. For my birthday, The Bell's parents gave me a card with the message 'be happy and *free*' inside it and The Bell spelt my name wrong in his rather peculiar offering of a twee Victorian street scene by the artist Anton Pieck. How romantic. Dad bought me a black and gold drop-waist dress and a bottle of Chanel No5. Mum sent along a message that she hoped I'd have 'a really horrible time'.

Anita's mother had done all the food for the party and the table looked lovely. Leda came dressed as Adam Ant in all the gear; she wore a big frilly shirt, Mum's fringed Red Indian moccasins and had painted a white stripe across her face. (When we had Sunday dinner over at Grandma's, Dad and my bother Kofi would impersonate Adam Ant's two drummers, beating out the rhythms on the table with their knives and forks.)

Loads of people turned up and got well out of it and they went on to sing Happy Birthday before spraying me liberally with canned string. Grandpa was chatting up my friends and then Grandma, wearing silver shoes and a black cape, berated him soundly for lurking about downstairs and taking pictures in the dark. She was not amused and she also asked us to turn the music down. 'Er Grandma, it's a twenty-first birthday party!'

The proceedings were somewhat marred by Dad, who had gone into a separate room to smoke loads of dope with his cronies and then he started playing his own music really loud. No, no, we want 'Ant Music.' However, my own list of music for the party was distinctly 'old hippy' I must say, The Ants stuff and The Police were supplemented by Hendrix, Doors, Beatles, Cream (!), Dire Straits (!!), Free and Bad Company. But then most of the people I was hanging out with were a few years older than me. The next day was my actual birthday and I worked in the morning. In the afternoon, all my lot from the flat took me out and got me ratted on triple Southern Comforts, which they were telling me were singles. Will I never learn? The snow had melted by New Years Eve and it became so foggy that Anita and I had difficulty even finding the familiar road, let alone getting over to Alex and Jayne's for a party.

CHAPTER TEN
Up the Junction: 1982

In January we had a load more snow, which coincided with the start of the Falklands War and I genuinely believed that conscription would return and all the men would be used up in World War Three. Although we quickly became aware that some guys did actually *want* to go. This was after The Bell gave a lift to a Squaddie hitching one night in Beaconsfield, who confided to him that he couldn't wait to get out there and 'start killing'. The Bell and I were struggling along, splitting up and getting back together again with great rapidity. Then in the midst of all this frozen uncertainty Dad and Number 2 announced that they were off to live in Italy, taking the two dogs and two remaining horses with them. (Piggy had been given to Phil the polo guy, who went on to neglect the old nag and left him out in a field to get full of worms. Happily for Pig, Brigitte our groom from the Ashton Wold times, managed to locate him, buy him back and care for him 'til the end of his days, which is bloody well done to her.)

Anyway, to say that I was a bit disappointed by this news of imminent departure is an understatement. I had followed gaily along, lured by the false promise of fun, fame and glory, discarding my education and any ideas I may have had about a career (none at all) along the way. Only to end up in mouldy bed-sit land in the middle of the country, picking up pooh all day and trying to have a relationship with a cold fish who liked doing his bank statements in bed! Never mind.

On the home front, Luis Basualdo had done a deal with The National Westminster bank to put a charge upon the house in Harrow. Mum had been awarded house and contents and a shilling a year in the divorce settlement, but at that time the wife was apparently liable for the husband's debts and the mortgage wasn't being paid. (In the sixties, you were encouraged to have a mortgage for tax purposes even if you could afford to buy your property and that house had only cost £13,000 in 1968). Dad was ordered to pay £36 p.w. for the upkeep of my two siblings, but he couldn't afford to. Meanwhile, Roy 'the getaway driver' sat happily in the front office of the recording studios at Acton, surrounded by Dad's gold discs and revelling in the fact that he now had power of attorney as he drove around town in a gold Mercedes.

Number 2 then got her own Dad to re-route any royalties through Hamburg so that Mum couldn't get her hands on any of it. On 30th January, Dad and Number 2 loaded up Dingbat the Land Rover and set off, only getting as far as Dover before they broke down. They rang Alex and asked him to come and help them. Alex's reply was something to the tune of, 'You are having a fucking laugh if you think I'm driving all the way to Dover to mend a car!' Then I had to look after Dad's remaining horses until a lorry turned up to take them on an adventure which would eventually see them ending their days in Denver, Colorado. The Bell was about as sympathetic to me as I was to any of his worries, which was not at all.

The job at Woodlands now also began to get a bit sticky. When you care for horses, you get attached to them and they think that they belong to you and not to some twonk who comes along with a saddle now and again and works the arse off them. Geoff's teenage daughter had this thuggish boyfriend whom she used to climb out of her bedroom window to go out with of an evening, with her carers being none the wiser. This boyfriend drove a yellow Vauxhall Victor and he had a Neanderthal-like family whom she would invite to come and muck around with the nags. If I got wind of their arrival, I would make sure I'd disappeared on a long ride so that their plans were thwarted. To add to this, the boy would get increasingly annoyed with his poor pony and want to put a stronger bit in its mouth, which resulted in me hiding it so that he couldn't. One horse became ill and the girl said I was making it up so she couldn't ride it, but I got the vet in and he confirmed my suspicions. This is what you're up against with people to whom owning an animal is a status symbol. I used to have a kip at lunchtime in the caravan there and this led them to believe that I didn't have enough work to do so Geoff asked me to go part time and I declined.

One April morning, not long before I left, I was mucking out as usual, when Alex turned up and informed me that I was the first to know that he and Jayne were now the proud parents of a baby girl born the previous night. They named her Nicola and whilst The Bell and I had the honour of becoming her Godparents, things were not going well for us. In fact we had one fight in which I packed his case and told him to bugger off, but then I changed my mind and sat on it so he couldn't leave. I also kicked him so hard on the shin that I made his leg bleed. So we split for a while and he started seeing the non-Goth one of the two Sarah's. She liked him a lot and bought him a watch, which made me furious.

I was beginning to change slowly and fashion-wise, I kept trying to do different things with my hair like backcomb it and over do the hair spray. I liked frilly shirts, heavier make-up and big earrings. I even put some pink streaks in my hair, but I was grooming for Mary Robbins at the time and she looked at me aghast and said, 'Oh! I do hope that's washed out by the time we go to Royal Windsor'. Something wasn't right somewhere.

A bloke named Peter had been seeing one of my mates and he asked me out one night. He took me to a Ricky Cool gig in Camden and he came in for coffee, but he didn't even try it on, how disappointing. I tried to get a life, but let's face it, I just wasn't in the right place to get the type of life I wanted, even if I had known what it was. I hated living alone and would just sit in the dark for hours staring at nothing and listening to the Phil Collins' 'Face Value' LP. I needed a cash injection from somewhere as my money (when I was still at Woodlands), wasn't lasting the week. So as well as sitting in the dark I had nothing to eat either and would have to go begging off Alan and Gayle. The Bell kept hanging about blowing hot and cold as only he knew how, so with unemployment looming I did a thing that I would never recommend, I issued him with an ultimatum. 'Either you make a commitment or you never see me again'

A short time later he appeared and sheepishly agreed that we could get engaged. The magical words at last. I was over the moon! I had joined the human race and would be normal like everybody else. I could walk around with a ring on my finger and the world would clearly see that somebody cared enough to be with me. It was a beautiful day early in May, when we set off to The New Forest Stallion Show with Mary Robbins. Everyone was full of congratulations, the sun was shining and although I briefly tasted happiness, it soon turned out to be a hollow victory. The Bell informed me that he must see the blonde Sarah that night in order to tell her it was all over between them. As we drove along the next evening towards the little ultra modern house he was now renting in Amersham, he let slip that he had slept with her as a farewell and that I was expected to sleep in the same bed. Like the wet wimp I was, I only insisted that he change the sheets. We then went over to some friends in Chalfont St Giles to 'celebrate' and they fed me so much Brandy and Babycham that I ended up lying in their front garden. We did receive quite a few cards and presents from our friends, but Mother & Father Bell never even mentioned it and pretended that it wasn't happening.

Then strangely enough, Sheryl from my school days invited us to a party over in Chingford. In September of 1977, she had married Roy from The Horseless crowd and she lived with him and their two children on the thirteenth floor of a (now demolished) tower block on The Chingford Hall Estate. As soon as I walked into the flat the first person I saw was Johnny Gale sitting on a chair by the window. Suburban Chingford was resplendent in its spring greenery behind him and the tall trees of the Forest marched upwards towards the clouds. He wore a close fitting dark jacket, he was smoking a cigarette and he didn't appear to be with anyone. By now he had reached the advanced age of thirty, which seemed very old to me. He looked different to my adult eyes and his hair was shorter, yet I still retained that memory of him at The Tower Flanagans, wearing his make up and tight trousers and tottering around his drum kit in white platform shoes.

So I moved into the house at Amersham for another short-lived idyll of domesticity. A young hippy friend named Phillip rented a room with us and he didn't take up much space because he'd lost all his possessions in two successive house fires. Yet he remained resolutely cheerful and unperturbed throughout. He was a sweet guy and I once asked him to remove a Daddy Long Legs from the living room wall. He approached it manfully, hesitated and then he turned to me and said with a wry smile, 'I don't like them either.' Phil later became another victim of the West Drayton dealers.

The healthy and ever ambitious Bell however, was a vegetarian and so I spent many hours making him vegetable pies with homemade brown pastry and other equally unappetising dishes. I had it down to a fine art and the moment he arrived home his dinner would be waiting for him on the table. In gratitude (!) he procured me some work at a riding school he was teaching at in Brawlings Lane, Seer Green. Initially I was detailed to clean out the old lady's larder for a tenner, because the ceiling had collapsed and items of food that had been there since World War Two had to be retrieved from under tons of plaster. After that, I began working there as a groom in the riding school, looking after vicious, over-worked nags that were even more miserable than the polo ponies. The head girl made me miss my lunch hour by clearing out a stable full of deep litter shavings, until the boss rescued me. It was awful. The Bell also took a leaf out of Dad's book and decided to use me as a free groom to look after his own horse, Fiddler.

Alex and Jayne had moved, along with his parents, to a farm just outside the village of Marsworth near Tring and The Bell and I, along with Fiddler and the two dogs, ended up living there too. Now I was very upset to be leaving that lovely, neat place in Amersham, but The Bell said he could not afford it, especially with my crappy earnings. Alex and Jayne had gone into a converted barn, in the roof of which was a space that had once been a grain loft and this could only be accessed by climbing up a ladder that came out of the ceiling and down the wall into their lounge. It was thick from floor to ceiling with dust up there, as well as being home to giant spiders, grey cobwebs and ancient piles of stale oats. There was no insulation at all and the winter wind whistled gaily through the gaps in the tiles. Welcome to my new home.

We employed poor Leda to start the cleaning, armed with an industrial vacuum cleaner and a facemask! I must say that I did enjoy living with Jayne, as it is unusual for two women sharing a kitchen to get on so well. But on the downside, The Bell and I argued continuously and I became increasingly aware of the resemblance the relationship was taking to that of my own parents (without the violence obviously). Then he accidentally collided with a motorcyclist's leg out on the road, resulting in yet another smashed up white Escort Van. *Then* he got done for another accident that involved him catching some overhead power cables with the back-actor on the tractor and not stopping to report the incident. He was quite distraught about all this, but as usual I was extremely 'unsympathetic'.

I got a job in 'The Angler's Retreat', which was the local pub situated at the end of our lane. I'd walk up there wearing the very same floral dress that I'd worn to The Horseless Carriage seven years before. I've always liked working behind a bar (home from home) and the Landlady was a nice woman whom I respected. She got me waitressing as well and I very much enjoyed flirting with 'The Canal Men' as I called them, because they were always very attentive. 'There's something about your eyes, they tell you things,' they used to say. Heavens! I would go home and look in the mirror to try and discover exactly what sort of things my eyes were suggesting to them without my knowledge.

I used to get paid £6 a session at the pub and The Bell very kindly let me keep it all, as I was saving up to go and see Dad and Number 2 in Italy. Anita was by then working as a ground hostess for British Airways, so she managed to procure good flights with upgrades to Club Class and we jetted off together that November for a holiday at Dad's rented place in Monte Morello near Pisa. Once there, we went sight seeing in Firenze, taking in the Ponte Vecchio and then eating white chocolate under the marble statue's extremely small willy. The eccentric guitarist, John Missaroli, was also visiting on that occasion and we had quite a laugh; but it was clear that Dad was if possible, even more skinto minto than I.

When I got back, The Bell had along with his mate Rupert, found work at a livery yard next to Park Farm called 'Batchworth' and so once again, we were on the move. This time I didn't mind upping sticks because we were going back to suburbia to live in Harrow. Hooray! We found a bed-sit at 175, Vaughan Road, just around the corner from my Grandmother's. The landlord of this establishment was a very odd fellow indeed named Michael, who wore clogs, drank Lucozade and always kept his eyes shut whilst addressing you. Strictly speaking, he said he only wanted girls there but The Bell must've turned on the charm to be allowed in. We also weren't allowed dogs either but we sneaked them in as well. Three other girls also lived there, and they were, Alison, Polly and Sheila, who were friendly and easy to get on with. Another slightly odd female occupant lived in a room under the stairs. A green light glowed there mysteriously and a strange boyfriend would come calling, with the result that we referred to her spooky abode as 'Igor's Green Grotto.' I was looking after Fiddler at Batchworth and I met a lovely girl called Sandra who kept her pony Sunny at livery there. She was scouting for somewhere to live and as luck would have it, Igor was on the move, so the wonderful Sandra came and joined us instead.

Outside the front door of 175 burned a red lamp, which caused us to say that it was secretly a brothel. A few years later, when we had long gone, the local newspaper carried an article showing the front door, complete with red light, informing the public that Michael 'you couldn't if you tried', had in fact recently been prosecuted for running a brothel on the premises. Obviously, he'd had plans for us of which we were blissfully unaware!

Although I did have some happy times with the girls, The Bell continued to get on my nerves with ever increasing frequency. I would assuage my resentment with small, undetected rebellions and I made the most of opportunities that came my way. Rather like the day that I'd made a sponge pudding for his dessert and left it out prior to putting it in the oven; when I came back to it later I noticed that one of Alison's cats had helped itself to a good portion, but I just smoothed it over with a smile, popped it in the oven and he was none the wiser.

CHAPTER ELEVEN
At the Crossroads: 1983

At 175 we settled in yet again and The Bell continued to work here and there, whilst I looked after Fiddler up at Batchworth; where a load of teenagers careered about on uncontrollable ponies and inevitably I became friendly with them. The stable next to mine was rented by a very effeminate but oddly sexy boy called Robert and we used to ride out together on summer days. Then Gothic Sarah came to work there and we used to go for lunch over at The Green Man pub across the road, where we were served with prawn rolls and coffee and biscuits by a very kindly lady. We also frequented the King's Road together on days off and bought killer stilettos (at last!) and crazy giant earrings from The Great Gear Market. I was always drawn to the group of hard-core punks who lurked moodily around the railings of a garden square. Once again I felt they epitomised freedom and identity.

Sarah and I took turns competing Fiddler in dressage competitions down at Park Farm and just like Abi before her, she was getting a bit of extra help from our old friend Mr Amphetamine Sulphate. Over a prawn roll she confided to me that whenever she closed her eyes at night, her bedroom became alive with scuttling rats, which disappeared whenever she switched the light on.

I said, 'Sarah, you are taking too much speed.'

'Oh, do you really think that's what it is?' she replied

incredulously.

She also warned me over and over that The Bell was seriously taking the piss and I suppose that eventually it did begin to sink in because when in that summer of 1983, The Bell informed me that he had decided he wanted us to move again as a better opportunity had presented itself to him out in the countrified wilds of somewhere or other; I said to him, 'You can move on your own, because I'm not doing it again.' I think he was a bit surprised, but after four and half years that was essentially the end of The Bell and I. I wouldn't be surprised if family Bell then went off and had a party to celebrate. Ding bloody dong.

Soon after that, I went out to Italy as Dad and Number 2 had decided to get married and a crowd of us stayed at the new farmhouse they had now moved to over at Larciano Castello. This place was half derelict but offered breathtaking views across a valley in which lights sparkled and mist rose as the sun set majestically behind the Dolomites. Sandra and Anita came out for the occasion along with my cousin Ken and a whole lot of Number 2's family. Sandra got persuaded into going out riding with Dad one day and he took her speeding along the sheer and narrow mountain paths in an unforgettable experience that she ever afterwards referred to as, 'The wall of death'!

The wedding took place in the local town of Prato and I wore a pink strapless dress overlaid with white lace, pink lace gloves and pink court shoes, whilst the bride wore a hideous mustard yellow ensemble overlaid with enormous black polka dots. After the ceremony we festooned Dingbat the Land Rover with shaving foam, ribbons and cans and we followed its noisy, smoking trail back to a reception party up at the house. (I last saw Dingbat sad and abandoned in an olive grove in 1988 and it wouldn't surprise me if it rusts there still.) The simple wedding cakes were adorned with pipe-cleaner representations of the happy couple that had passport photos for faces, and the crotch of Dad's effigy was symbolically tied up with a pink ribbon.

As the evening wore on, I got severely molested by a Yank and it was like being attacked by an octopus. I managed to get rid of him eventually but then he started on Anita and she was not amused.

Anita was also not at all amused when we got back to London and I urged her to come with me to see the film Mad Max II. I'd been intrigued by the trailers and had decided that Mel Gibson in black leather was something that I needed to see. Anita however, was unable to stomach the violent content of the film and was horrified that I had subjected her to it. Quite clearly we had suddenly become miles apart. She could drive and owned a car; she had a career and prospects, whilst I drifted about with no money and no direction at all. The scene was being set for an inevitable parting of the ways.

For a while, Fiddler the horse stayed at Batchworth where I continued to care for him and I also got a bit of work there, but not much. Then there was a big hoo ha up at the yard that was caused by two middle-aged women doing some stirring and it turned around as though it was all my doing. The boss cornered me one day and told me that The Bell had assured her that I would be gone by the end of October, but of course he had not told me. It all got a bit heated to put it mildly and The Bell took poor old Fiddler off to a life of God knows what until his demise.

The Bell was constantly pressing to me to sign on the dole to get money and my Dad was also keen on the idea. 'I've paid more tax than most people earn in a lifetime, so go and get some of it back,' was his mantra.

As with all options presented to me, I wavered for a

while because I felt it was tantamount to admitting you were a lost cause and belonged to a proletariat underclass of no hoper. In other words, I was a Snob. But I swallowed my pride and forged the beginnings of a life long romance with the warm safety net of the wonderful welfare state.

'Feel no pain, no pain
No regret, no regret.
When the line's been signed
You're someone else
Do yourself a favour, the meal ticket does the rest.'
(Elton John: *'(Gotta get a) Meal Ticket')*

I had some money, but now I needed romance. I still went to visit Alan and Gayle quite regularly and they had recently moved to a flat overlooking the common at Chalfont St Peter. The Baker's Arms had been renamed The Poachers by now, and I would go there with them hoping to catch a glimpse of some Carp or other in order to brighten up my increasingly doomy existence. Sometimes Jimmy would pop in and say 'hello', which always gave me a buzz and then one night, I was standing at the bar when Dave walked in behind me. Just hearing his voice made my mouth go dry and my knees turn to jelly and the world fairly crackled and fizzed with electricity, desire and joy. In less than thirty seconds I was hooked again. Oh, if only I could get him. I decided to have a party at Vaughan Road and I actually got Dave and Jimmy to come along, a feat indeed, as it was quite a long way from their home turf. I wore the dress Dad had bought me for my twenty-first, but this time with fishnet tights and spiky stilettos, coupled with back combed hair, huge earrings and fingerless lace gloves. Dave arrived, got pretty out of it and became a sitting target for me. *'Before you slip into unconsciousness, I'd like to have another kiss...'* (Crystal Ship: The Doors)

I spent the entire evening draped over the poor guy. At the end though, much to my utter despair, Jimmy dragged him away and by doing so he inadvertently saved my life.

Then I went to see the film 'Breathless', starring Richard Gere and I thought he looked so like Dave that I was filled with longing. Dave did actually call me after that and he agreed to come over to Harrow to take me out one night. I really thought I'd made it and I got ready that evening with great care and attention to detail. I wore a white frilled shirt with a knee length, flared, mauve cord skirt and high heels, which I'm sure looked pretty terrible, then I poured myself a drink and I waited. I poured myself another drink and I smoked some fags and had another drink and the bottle is finished and Dave my dears, is not coming and has stood me up. I can't say I was all that surprised. In hindsight of course I know my life was saved once more, but to be quite honest, at that time I would rather have had Dave and died, so pass the tissues. Sob!

I went to Italy once more that December and I took the train home through the Swiss Alps just before Christmas. A young New Zealand guy was sharing my compartment and he was okay but a totally unattractive speccy four-eyes type. I chatted to him because it was nice to speak English to someone after having to get by on my crap Italian. He suggested we turn the carriage lights out in order to get the full benefit of the breathtaking spectacle of chocolate box chalets nestling in the snow with glittering Christmas trees lit up beside them. It was an unforgettable sight, but as we settled down to sleep, his voice came down to me out of the darkness and asked, 'Miss Baker, would you like a cuddle?'

'No thanks!'

Well it could only happen to me, the woman with 'creeps please apply here' tattooed on her forehead but I suppose that on his part it was worth a try.

Then I got a crush on the guitarist of a band that my brother was in. This bloke ran a music shop in Wembley and was a complete dork, but for a while I liked him because he played hard to get, which in other words means he wasn't interested. So I had a birthday party and found myself French kissing him in the hallway of the house whilst the orange glare of the street light streamed in upon us through the open door. A door through which he escaped with some alacrity!

> The street outside was empty
> The cold wind gave a sigh
> And my voice it sounded foolish
> So reluctant for goodbye

Yes I wrote as much depressing poetry as possible.

> Across an icy waste, it's half past ten
> Fingers frozen, will I look up again?
> Across unmoving years, I forget my lines
> Lips are moving, but I cannot read the signs.

And I headed towards a Christmas period that I predicted would consist only of interminable hours of loneliness.

It *was* pretty grim, and still ranks among the worst that I have ever had. On Christmas Eve, I went down to The John Lyon with Sean. I wore a green crocheted dress that had been made for me some time previously by my Nan and I teamed it with fishnet tights, grey stilettos and earrings made out of enormous pieces of bent green Perspex. At this point, I was only a short way along the Punk path. The John Lyon crew being 'Casuals' were not really ready for this sort of spectacle, however tame. They even had enormous difficulty in coping with the Perspex earrings for Christ's sake.

Yes, I was with the wrong people and I knew it, but where were the right ones? My old love, the air rifle toting, cat shooting, Loony appeared out of the woodwork along with his latest victim. Much to her chagrin he made a great fuss of me and said, 'I love you and you are wonderful, you will be happy one day I know it'... etc, etc. Oh go away and boil your head! There was not one man there who interested me and to top it all I had a wisdom tooth coming through, so I sought solace in painkillers and booze. After several million whiskies and glasses of red wine I was invited off somewhere for a smoke. I finally arrived home without my handbag, I had a hole in my fishnets and then I was sick.

When the daylight crept in it illuminated only me lying on top of the bed still fully clothed. I slowly regained consciousness and thought, 'Shit! It's Christmas Day!'
Then I had to stagger round to my grandmother's and have lunch with four people over the age of eighty, which when you're only 23 is a bit depressing, especially as the conversation consisted of an endless litany of aches and pains. But by the New Year, my self indulgent misery was starting to bore even me and when I got introduced to a girl who was more mind numbingly negative than I was, I swore to myself then and there that I was seriously going to get a grip. That is when I stepped back from the abyss.

CHAPTER TWELVE
All Tomorrow's Parties: 1984

*'Loving would be easy if your
colours were like my dreams...'*
(Culture Club: 'Karma Chameleon')

T he heavy Orwellian connotations that the date implied weren't lost on me. The Thatcher regime felt oppressive to those of us with no money or possessions and not a lot of hope of getting them (i.e. lazy buggers). Things were changing and a lot of creative young people felt compelled to express themselves in the sub culture that flourished in suburbia. Of course it is well known that harder regimes can foster greater creativity and political awareness, but I didn't know this at the time.

My looks were also under going constant modifications in response to the shifting sands that I found myself cast out upon. My teeth, that in the far away days of Johnny Gale and The Horseless Carriage had just come out of braces and looked even and straight, had continued their outward trajectory over the years at an alarming rate. By the time I was eighteen, four snaggly tombstones stood alone practically at right angles to my gum and no flowery girly attire on earth was going to complement this defect. A more aggressive look definitely suited both me and my funny face.

At the beginning of March, I went a little further and dressed up for a party at the new bed-sit that Sheila from

175 had recently moved into in Edgware. Apparently they threw a party at that address every year and this was the first time that it hadn't been graced by the presence of George Michael because he was getting too famous. But although I didn't get to see Mr Michael in the flesh, I did meet a tall and graceful boy who reminded me very much of my friend Robert, from the yard at Batchworth. This guy was called Richard and he possessed that peculiarly girly, dark and high cheek boned charm that I was starting to find increasingly attractive. Boy George and Marilyn were racing up the charts along with the lovely Marc Almond in his eyeliner. As with Johnny Gale back in '75 I immediately responded to this latent streak of sexual ambiguity. Marilyn especially embodied my perfect ideal, the combination of the masculine body and the beautiful, made-up face.

And here my penchant I disgorge
For men like Marilyn and George.

Who cares if they were all gay? Because it wasn't long before I discovered many who weren't. Anyway back in Edgware, I soon pounced on my unwary victim and was immediately entangled in a breathless heap for the duration. I was so impressed that I wrote this poem.

I watched this morning's dawn
come through a skylight on a landing,
Where I was with my head laid upon a stranger's breast.
And I had cast off all my burdens
and found at last contentment,
And I knew that this was really the great pinnacle of rest.
Then as the time came for my leaving,
I tried to gather up my feelings

That I'd poured out on to someone
   that I didn't even know-
The joy of giving after loneliness,
   the ecstasy of tenderness,
The feeling of belonging when
   there's no place left to go.
And I left him still a stranger,
   sitting in a grey-lit kitchen,
With a murmur and a wonder
   if we once again might meet?

And he sat there with my feelings
   as I staggered into daylight
And waited at the bus-stop
   in the early morning sleet.

We *did* meet again, but not for quite a while. In the meantime, I got very cold in the bed-sit and I was fiddling the meter in order to get enough heat. In the end I gave up any pretence of fending for myself and moved in with Grandma and Grandpa round the corner. The Bell was still hovering about and he pushed me into getting a job at a riding school down at Manston in Kent. This was an unmitigated disaster and I can't imagine why I ever allowed myself to be talked into it. I think it was the idea of getting £50 per week, which seemed a lot then. I had to stay in a little frozen caravan and the toilet was ten yards away in the woods. I had to muck out stables piled up to the roof with shit and lead children on ponies round an outdoor school that was knee deep in mud.

The telephone box was about a mile up the road and all the other girls talked about was getting off with the guys from the Air Force base. Help! After three days, I pretended I was going to see a relative in Chatham and got the bloke there to give me a lift to the station. I took my dog, my jewellery box and as much else as I could carry and went back to West Harrow. I stood on Finchley Road Tube Station (the stop I had used for school), looked up at the hoardings and felt elated to be free once more. My aunt and uncle in Bexley very kindly went and collected the rest of my stuff.

Just after that, Alison from 175 asked me to go to a gig up at Warwick University with her. This is where she'd done her degree and she was anxious to hook up with a man she'd had a thing with on the campus there. I wore the twenty-first birthday dress yet again and was soon abandoned by Alison who'd gone off to do naughty things somewhere in halls. I wandered about and sat down to watch a band that turned out to be 'The Bluebells' and jolly good they were too. I also tried unsuccessfully to chat someone up. In the early hours, Alison reappeared and was so tired that she asked me (who hadn't passed my test) to drive her Lada back down the motorway whilst she crashed out in the back. I woke her up when we got to Greenford and driving called for a more competent approach.

At the end of the month, I went out and managed to bag another bloke at a party. This was a skinny blond thing with long luxuriant curls who wore tight trousers, listened to loud Heavy Metal music and drove around very fast in a black Reliant Robin. He also had a big motorbike, his name was Russell and he asked me out. I was thrilled; things were looking up at last. Or were they? Russell never wanted sex but he did once give me so many love bites on my neck that I couldn't turn my head. On the plus side, he also had a couple of nice friends called Bill and Jo.

Once again, I tried to go and look for a decent paying

job in normal land. I always enjoyed the getting dressed up for the interview bit and chatting away about myself. However, it became clear that no one was interested in a ballet dancing horse rider with three O'Levels, who couldn't type and was hopeless at maths and they did have a point. But The Bell had been working for a woman who was at that time seen as a demi-god in the Dressage world. She held an FBHS, which is the horse equivalent of a Phd. Under normal circumstances, she would never have considered taking on someone who had no formal qualifications, but she was in such dire straits staff wise (because she couldn't pay them), that The Bell convinced her to give me a try. I went off to this beautiful Georgian Mansion in Stokenchurch, where she had use of their stable yard. This picturesque village is home to the windmill where they made the film 'Chitty Chitty Bang Bang' apparently.

When I arrived, the other girls regarded me with suspicion and the whisper went around that I couldn't possibly be a horsey person because my nails were too long. But long nails or not, I could muck out (how hard is it?) and that basically was what was required. The Equestrian avatar requested that I continue to sign on and that she would pay me £10 per week to work six thirteen hour days with a half hour lunch break. In return for that, I'd get the odd lesson with her on the Grand Prix horse (this means it is highly skilled and NOT that it is capable of a top speed of 220 mph) and also get to ride the advanced horses from time to time. To be honest, it was in that respect a good opportunity and helped me in ways that have been of no earthly use to me whatsoever.

I moved in to a little mobile home that was hidden in a barn in order to avoid the prying eyes of local council planning officers. In the mornings, the other girls and I would sing loudly together as we mucked out, mainly to tapes of either Culture Club's 'Colour By Numbers' or Lionel Richie's latest LP (*'Hello, is it me you're looking for?'*) and I have to say that with practice, even my terrible singing voice did improve. We looked after a few horses that were supposed to be 'having therapy', you might say. One of these belonged to none other than Angie Best (former wife of George), who would often appear with her rich American businessman boyfriend in tow. The head girl was a lovely person called Tracey who for some inexplicable reason changed her name to Jade during my time there. She was a gem to work with and pulled her weight and then some, which is an attitude you don't come across that often. She was also having an affair with a married bloke and one night she inveigled me in to staying in her room in the mansion so that no one would realise she was out and I spent a fraught night sneaking about with my dog trying to make sure my presence went undetected.

I was still seeing blond Russell and would walk up to the phone box to speak to him and then go and swoon my life away believing it was all hunky dory, whilst planning my wedding and my bridesmaids outfits. On my day off, I'd walk up to the bus stop, then I'd get the coach back to Harrow and go out to The Plough in Kenton on Thursday nights when a local band called The Bozos would play. We had got to know them because my sister had started seeing one of their mates; a much older hippie guy named Phil. Before I did the journey back again to Stokenchurch, Leda and I would walk the dog by the lake on Harrow Hill and on one occasion he must have imbibed a quantity of brackish water, because he produced a vast amount of black sick on the floor of the coach and the driver threw me off to wait for the next one.

The Bell by the way had started seeing a horsey friend of mine and one night they took me with them to a party at Alex and Jayne's. I wasn't too thrilled at having to see her cosying up to all our mutual friends and I proceeded to get extremely lairy and well out of it. On the way back they had to stop the car to let me throw up and then I had to stay at The Bell's place with them in one room and me dying of drink and self-pity in another. Get the violins out. Although I was very much into Russell, it became clear that he in no way reciprocated. We'd been out somewhere and were sat in Grandma's driveway on a night in May that was heavy with the scent of newly opened roses blooming in their suburban flowerbeds.

I must've said, 'Is it worth going on?'

And he must've said, 'No it isn't', because that was the end of that.

I lay in bed as the silver trains clattered back and forth outside my window and I experienced the familiar sense of void and loss. I told myself that I must get used to this feeling as I was bound to meet it on many more occasions. But of course it's the same every time.

I still saw Russell a lot socially as I was friendly with his sister and with Bill and Jo. Bill used to take me out to lunch sometimes and it was he who told me that Russell had informed him that he'd only asked me out because he felt sorry for me and he thought I didn't get out much due to the fact that I was so ugly. This makes me laugh a lot, but at the time it was a bit of a low blow.

Then Polly from 175, moved into a studio flat further up Vaughan Road and she kept bumping into this really good looking builder who was working on a new development called Badger's Close just around the corner. It didn't take long before she was seeing him and we all went around together. His name was John and he was a classically handsome guy with long, brown, David Cassidy style hair, brown eyes and a typical builder's wit. He was always 'mad for the ride' and he had an identical twin brother who was a sparks (electrician), called David. Now whilst John was rampantly heterosexual in every respect, the beautiful David was unashamedly very gay indeed.

They began to join our scene, which now included Leda and Phil and all of his friends, 'the hippies of Harrow'. This dodgy lot were about ten years my senior and were seriously dedicated to hard drinking, casual sex and smoking copious amounts of dope, enlivened now again by the odd sprinkling of coke and acid. I felt privileged to finally meet up with the originators of the witty local graffiti that had formed part of my childhood. On many occasions in the 'seventies, I had come home from school laughing, after spotting their hilarious daubs from the top deck of a 182 bus. This was proper graffiti, which to my mind had some sort of cultural resonance, as opposed to unintelligible 'tagging' hieroglyphs. The roundabout at Northwick Park gave us, *'Nicholas Parsons is the neo-opiate of the people'* for years, as well as the brilliant *'Acid Frees the Mind'*, which was soon corrupted to, *'Acid Fries the Mind.'* A now defunct block of flats up by Roxborough Bridge proclaimed *'Your Logic is a Dog and so am I'*, alongside *'Smoke Lots of Pips Get High.'* These last two apparently having been composed by the legendary Dennis (more about him later).

You couldn't fail to notice that leafy Harrow had become home to a thriving community of young people, who began to respond collectively to the changes in their environment that were being brought about by the impending destruction of the town centre. Yes, poor old Harrow was on its way to becoming the soulless sham devoid of culture that most of our town centres now are, but during this painful transition, a great period of creativity ensued. The empty shops were squats where parties happened and houses awaiting the bulldozer offered cheap accommodation to youngsters starting out on their own. Stragglers and rag tags soon drifted in lured by a new sense of youth and freedom and this mini community with its very own sub-culture began to flourish. Naturally, I wanted to be part of it and out in Stokenchurch I felt cut off. Then a couple of things occurred that helped to set me on a new course.

Although I had been riding longer than The Bell, he was keen for me to understand that he was far more skilled at it than I and whenever he was teaching anywhere and I went along, he'd bung me in the Novice class. I never really voiced any resentment; I just thought, 'Perhaps I am useless'. But one fine day in Stokenchurch, I was having a lesson on the Grand Prix stallion and being taught by the demi-god lady, when she said the most extraordinary thing. She told me that I had 'feel' and that if I worked very hard I could be very good and she wasn't wholly complimentary about The Bell. I could have fallen off with surprise. I know it sounds particularly boring for someone non-horsey, but to me it was a very big deal indeed. That one small sentence did wonders for my self-esteem. I don't know if it were true, or only so much flannel, but very much later someone else very good told me the same thing, so who knows? However, rather than it making me think, 'Hooray I will now work hard to be brilliant', I felt as though I had nothing more to prove in that direction, that if I had a gift then I could go back to it if I felt I passionately needed to and I was *not* (and never had been) passionate about horse life. I had always loathed the heavy physical work, coupled with being squashed and stepped on and having to look like a scarecrow all the time. I didn't feel the need to prove anything to the world, only to myself and I looked around me at young people who in my opinion were working their arses off for nothing and missing out on real life as a result. I began to seriously question what it was that I imagined I was doing.

The second insight came on a gloriously still May evening. I sat in the caravan and looked out onto rolling green meadows in which tall and graceful horse chestnut trees held up their great white candles to the sky. At that very moment, I expected Michael Praed in full Robin Hood garb with his long flowing hair and his leather trousers laced up the sides, to appear and carry me off to another dimension. In a way he did, because just over a week later I packed up my stuff and got the coach back to suburbia to become in my own words, 'A full time purple-haired dosser.'

> *'...away from all we know,*
> *That's where I want to go,*
> *Out on the wild side...'*
> (ELO: 'Wild West Hero)

And I know I should be quoting Lou Reed instead here about shaving legs and he's being she's, but this just shows you how middle of the road I really am!

Anyway, the first thing I did with my new found freedom was to get the hair dye out and things took off immediately. I went to Beccy fair with the Alex and Jayne gang and nabbed The Bell for a bit of much needed sex without his girlfriend noticing (she wasn't there). It was still terrible but it's the thought that counts. Then my young friend Robert got in touch and we went off to Pinner Fair together. We scandalised all the other teenagers from Batchworth by snogging in front of them on the opposite platform at Pinner Station. He was still a girly and gangly sixteen and I was twenty-three, so I restrained myself from taking things further and he soon went back to Hampshire where he was working.

I continued my socialising with the handsome twins, in particular with David to whom I became quite close. David lived in a Victorian cottage on the lower slopes of the Hill and the other twin John soon moved in to one of the newly built cottages in Badgers Close. Fortunately for the twins, their older brother was a local developer who was cashing in the housing boom, so consequently they nearly always had work and somewhere to live. David lavished time, money and attention upon me and I spent a lot of time with him and his gay friends.

They took me out to the Euston Tavern, where I would dance and enjoy the drag acts, so I suppose you could say that for quite a while I became a Fag Hag. We used to listen to Streisand and Joni Mitchell, (*'I wish I had a river I could skate away on'*) and get maudlin. David had a dark side that I liked. He also enjoyed taking me out and pretending that I was his girlfriend, though I have to say that it didn't do much for my own chances. Together, the twins were an entertaining double act and while we laughed over David's camp and cutting wit, John would get jealous and come in doing something ridiculous, such as a waiter's juggling act, which involved several glasses that he had sellotaped to a tray. Or David would go out and buy new gear and then shortly after discover that John was wearing it all. Then by complete coincidence their mother turned out to be the lovely lady who used to serve prawn rolls to Sarah and I when we'd had our daily lunches in The Green Man.

Now instead of mucking out, I spent my days raiding

the local library and reading about the lives of the British monarchs, beginning with The Saxon Kings and working my way through until I got to Queen Victoria. I could also be very odd and take out sociology books by choice, such as wordy overviews of life in medieval England and anthropological studies of the nineteenth-century East End. I read fluffy novels and biographies of those who had flared brightly and died alone in booze or drug filled degradation. I got into Oscar Wilde's *'Portrait of Dorian Gray'* and subsequently I devoured his poetry. I wholeheartedly empathised and identified with his ideological position on the relinquishing of everything for sensation and I related to the notion of *'feasting with panthers.'* I even got out Walter Greenwood's *'Love on the Dole'* to see if he could offer me a few pointers. And almost every night if we could muster the funds we went pubbing and at the weekends it was any excuse for a party. From now on these were parties that were always packed and nobody gave a flying fuck what you wore, what you did for a living, where you came from, how old you were or even what your name was as long as you liked a drink, a smoke, a laugh, a good dance and getting off with people.

On 2nd June, John decided to have a moving in party for his place in Badgers Close. His relationship with Polly was faltering because she was quite an intense lady and he was always 'mad for the ride' with as many attractive women he could find and there was no shortage of takers. The party was going to be packed and we all eagerly anticipated the event. I wore some tight cut off jeans with a very see through white Edwardian shirt I'd had for years, the inevitable stilettos on my feet and bits of pink net tied in my hair. Russell appeared at the party and I had a swoon. In fact, I was still seeing quite a bit of him and he had even taken me up to a pub in Windsor with him one night on the back of his 1000cc motorbike. Obviously he continued to labour under the misapprehension that I didn't get out that much. Then The Bell and his latest squeeze turned up and they expressed horror at my Pinner Fair dalliance with young Robert. Bill, who was standing near me, took one look at The Bell's girl and said, 'Who'd leave a palace to live in a council house?' Which was a nice thing to say but unfortunately Russell didn't share that opinion.

However, one of my Mum's workmates did ask me to go home with him, but he had no chance because he was way too normal looking for me. The party roared on, Russell went home alone and I of course got very, very, drunk. I was constantly being hassled by Leda's boyfriend Phil, who was desperate to inform me that his friend in the corner really fancied me. In the end I said, 'Well, which one is he then?' and Phil pointed him out.

I saw a tall-ish, not bad looking bloke with dark hair and if it's not bad, getting late and a dead cert how can you refuse? So I brazenly set about a quick chat up, not expending too much energy as I was guaranteed a success. He asked me if I'd like to go home with him and I said, 'I'm not on the pill [I'd come off it thinking my sex life was over] and I have to bring my dog'. He coped with this okay. Off we went and I didn't even know his name, only that Phil had referred to him as 'Five'.

Dawn was breaking over Harrow as we drove down the Hill to the lights at the Greenford Road junction. I felt both apprehensive and liberated as I contemplated the adventure I was now on. This 'Five' bloke was ten years older than me and I was treated to a most welcome experience after all those years of The Bell. As a Jilly Cooper character says in her short story 'A Pressing Engagement', *'It was like hearing "The Merry Peasant" strummed out for years on an out-of-tune, upright piano, then suddenly having it played by Arthur Rubenstein on a Bechstein'.*

The next morning, he dropped me home and asked me for my phone number, which I felt reluctant to give, but I wrote it for him on a scrap of paper with the crumbling charcoal of a spent match.

'By the way,' I said breezily as I got out of the van, 'What's your name?'
And the answer, not at all heavy with tales of impending heartbreak, was 'Dennis.'

When he didn't phone me I began to get interested and then when Phil informed me that Dennis didn't 'want any ties' that made me more interested still. A couple of Thursdays later, I met him on a drunken night up The Plough. Dutch courage enabled me to go over and speak to him and he bought me a drink, before we all went off to The Tandoor for more partying. The Tandoor was an Indian restaurant on the bridge that spans the railway lines at Harrow Met. The proprietor lived near me in West Harrow and he knew us all so when it got late he'd lock the doors and we'd bring our own music tapes to play and just generally dance and party in there. After we'd done this, we went back to Dennis's gaff in Greenford and you won't be very surprised to learn that I ended up staying the night. If only I'd known what I had been missing, but maybe it would've been better if I hadn't.

I did some research and discovered that he had experienced a failed romance with one of the other girls in the crowd. They had apparently been an item for ages and he was in love, but after a while she left him for the curly haired, lead singer of The Bozos, whom she later married. Yet they still all socialised together and nobody appeared to get upset or even mentioned it, which I thought was odd and Dennis was quite clearly devastated by this defection. He was also a hopeless drunk. How he kept his job going I'll never know, for he was very often to be seen collapsed in a heap somewhere, or falling into things and nobody said anything about that either because he was a deity from the inner sanctum and commanded vast amounts of respect from all his associates.

Around this time his father became ill and died, which I suppose can't have improved his state of mind. What further information did I need? He easily fitted the bill of requirements in that he was a tortured individual who only needed to experience my wonderfulness in order to be cured, so I fell in love and poor Dennis grabbed his alcohol and headed for the hills. If he ignored me then there were very many other fairly ropey looking women that he took home with him and they were often chasing after him or holding him up as he swayed about uncertainly. I don't know where he found them.

Nevertheless, I wasn't too downhearted because I was busy making friends and I accrued a couple or three creepy admirers of my own who offered me what they thought I wanted but sadly I didn't want it from them. It was a large crowd and merely going out of your front door meant that you bumped into people you knew or had seen around. They waved and shouted and offered lifts in cars and camper vans and went round to each other's houses to drink tea and skin up and talk about '*life the universe and everything*'.

They had nicknames like Wozzo, Pogo, Pom, Topper, Shuggy and Legs. We usually drank in The Roxborough and The Castle up on Harrow Hill, where there was a grumpy landlord named Morris and after the pub of course, there was The Tandoor. We went to see The Bozos in The Plough every Thursday and there was another place in Watford called The Pumphouse, where bands would play on Sunday afternoons. I still saw a lot of Alison and I also became close to Sandra who worked in Barclay's Bank in Harrow. Her colleagues would always have a good laugh at my appearance whenever I went in to meet her for lunch.

The town continued to buzz and I was now working on getting myself in with the hallowed inner circle, in which of course, Dennis was one of the leading lights. At the same time, I had my eye firmly on the punks who could often be seen walking over the Roxborough Bridge and flaunting their increasingly outlandish hairdos. I wondered how I could get to know them? I found a hairdressers called 'Memory Lane' and Emma the stylist there, suggested that she put the clippers up the sides of my head for my first step towards the great mohican. I was more than happy to let her do her thing. We started to frequent some of the punk gigs that were being held in the basement music venue of The Roxborough pub, but I still felt that their music was akin to Mr Angry's night out.

The twins were still very much on the scene and I was round at David's a lot. A bloke we knew called 'Shaggy Bill' lived in the flats next door to him and we were often in there as well. 'Shaggy Bill' said he thought that my style was comparable to that of Vivienne Westwood and as I had no idea who she was then I didn't know if that was a compliment or not. One night Bill came over and we all got very out of order, drunk and smashed; we lit exploding cigarettes, put washing up liquid in our coffee and then John and Bill went and nicked the hub caps off a car that belonged to a woman from over the road. Then David threw us out so we went over to Bill's where I couldn't even work the kettle to make the tea and poured cold water into the cups.

Yes, I was quite interested in Shaggy Bill, but when I asked John what he thought my chances were he said, 'Nought'. Oh well. When we got back, Leda was being silly and began turning the landing light on and off whilst singing 'diddle I, diddle I' in reference to a Scottish bloke who was after me. Usually we'd be so overcome with the munchies when we got in late that we'd raid Grandma's cake tin and get the hysterical giggles. Grandma was always delighted that we enjoyed her baking so much.

I had begun to get friendly with Mum again after our long estrangement and a whole troop of us often went back over to the old house for Sunday dinner with her. The place had started to get a bit run down and what with that and us funny looking poor folks turning up on the doorstep all the time, the snooty neighbours were getting a bit concerned. She had also been having a few adventures of her own in my absence.

I've already mentioned that due to Dad's defection and the strange terms of the ensuing acrimonious divorce, the mortgage wasn't being paid, so the previous winter when Mum had been on the dole she had found herself unable to pay the gas bill. One day a policeman had arrived with the Gas Board to cut her off. 'This is a warrant, that's if you can read' he rather unwisely said to Mum. I say unwisely, because any member of my family will tell you that that sort behaviour results in getting a thick ear and that is precisely what happened to Mr Plod.

In a trice he had whipped out his handcuffs and carted her off to Wembley nick and once she had been charged, they made her walk back to Harrow with no shoes on in the middle of November. Wankers. A few months later, a posse of bailiffs turned up to try and evict her and my two younger siblings. No one was in at the time, so they changed the locks, but my brother soon arrived and clambering up on to the conservatory roof he broke back in again through his own bedroom window.

Mum eventually managed to get a job with a well-known double-glazing firm at their showroom in Neasden and she got in with the local villains and spent long hours drinking with them in the smoky environs of the Neasden Wine Bar. She also got me a bit of work from time to time, manning a stall in Wembley covered market or answering the phones on a Saturday when the showroom was empty. God knows what prospective customers thought when they were confronted with me, but her bosses were happy to give me twenty quid for a day spent sitting there reading my book, so God bless them.

At the end of June in normal land, my friend Janet gave birth to a baby boy and in weirdo country we all decided to go off to Glastonbury Festival. Alex and Jayne had decided to run a stall there, so Jayne and I went in her Ford Escort and picked up a friend along the way, then we followed Alex who was manfully towing an over loaded caravan with the Land Rover. It was hot when we arrived and set up the stall, but we started selling our wares straight away and a couple came up that were completely naked. Nobody said a word until they'd gone and then we wet ourselves laughing like little kids. Opposite us was a clothes stall, one of whose members was a willowy young boy, who with his dark hair hanging in his eyes, reminded me of Robert and so I spent a lot of time leering over him discreetly.

The Bell and Dee arrived together followed by John and David and then I met up with the rest of the Harrow crowd that included my sister and her new man Tony. He was a tall bleached blond with not much of a face but a body like you wouldn't believe. She had by now split amicably from Phil, who like John 'the builder' went on to bed almost every girl he met in a determined yet good-natured fashion, causing mayhem in his wake. My brother Kofi now appeared at our caravan and gaily recounted a story of how he had witnessed a hippy girl drop her tray of hash fudge all over the ground and then went on to describe the way in which he had proceeded to liberate some of it into his own stomach. As a result of this marvellous piece of petty pilfering, he crashed out in his tent and wasn't seen or heard of again for two days.

On the Friday evening, the rest of us danced the night away to the sounds of Ian Dury and The Blockheads and on the Saturday, I bumped into a close friend of Alan's and I also met up with Graham Bond's widow Dianne as I pushed through the crowd in front of Elvis Costello. Once again, I was part of an all-encompassing community of like-minded freaks and I found it very comforting. On the Sunday, we all sat in a big circle near the beer tent, communing companionably in the sun and Dennis came loping slowly towards us out of the trees. He was wearing wrap around mirror shades; a cut away sleeveless vest and he had an axe slung carelessly over his shoulders. His biceps bulged and I very quietly died of longing and desire.

Later that night, Leda and I headed back towards our tent, both totally out of it. At a point where many tracks converged we argued about the correct route back past endless tents all looking much the same in the gloom. She adamantly set off on her own path, so I said, 'Bye' and went off on my way. Throngs of people congregated outside various wigwams having mini parties, with fires and candles burning, their music competing with that of the camp next door. Laughter rang out and everywhere the air was heavy with dope smoke. Drunken shadows lurched endlessly back and forth, swearing and singing and tripping over guy ropes as they passed. I got back to the tent and settled into my sleeping bag nursing that condition peculiar to such events that I call 'festival lip' (this is when you've smoked so many hot roaches that your bottom lip gets a blister). Half an hour later, the zip opened and Leda came stumbling in. 'Have a nice walk?' said I, 'Fuck off!' said Leda.

We went home the next day to a much-needed bath and grandma's cooking. A couple of nights later after a long smoking session with David I got in at about four in the morning and the birds were singing joyously. It had become such a perfect life that I could now indulge myself in the memory of Dennis. So I sat in my little bed by the window and as the first pale light of dawn filtered through the chinks in the pink satin curtains I wrote this:

> The Birds sing in an amber dawn
> That brings a silver crescent moon
> Hanging Silmarillion bright
> In the mists that all too soon
> Will lift, and give us morning light
>
> I saw him last in some vast field
> Where thousands sat with souls at play
> And resting smiles lazed in the sun.
> My dreams blossomed and blew away
> His heart untouched by every one.
>
> In this room a light burns brightly
> Whilst day creeps through the curtains drawn,
> Too much past and no tomorrow
> When there's a chance to be reborn
> Why must I be a friend to sorrow?

At the end of July, Mum had been invited to go along to the International Polo up at Windsor and she wanted me to go with her. Oh dear. I wasn't that keen on the idea as I had by now left that world far behind me and I knew that they would all die when they saw by my attire just what direction I was now heading in. Nevertheless, I got ready on that warm morning determined to make an impact. I wore the old purple cord skirt, and very high grey snake effect stilettos. On my top half I had on a black see-through lace vest and no bra. My burgundy coloured hair was back-combed and lacquered up very high.

Firstly, we were taken to the house in Winkfield Row where I had looked after our horses in early '77. It was full of important Nigerians who were apparently horrified by my appearance. When we arrived at Smith's Lawn all the Paparazzi asked me if I was a Right Honourable somebody, because otherwise how could I have got in? I saw all my old friends but every one of them completely ignored me except for Charlie Graham and Gig Horswell. I was quite frankly appalled by the whole atmosphere and I felt them to be nothing but plastic people whose seemingly mindless social climbing concerns were very far apart from my own, but perhaps I was only jealous. When we finally got back to Harrow that evening I went straight up to The Castle and was so delighted to be back on my home turf, that I flirted outrageously with one of my little old admirers and made his day!

Leda then set off travelling about on the hippy festival circuit. She went to Stonehenge and The Elephant Fayre down in Cornwall. Whilst she was there a punk guy (who coincidentally happened to be one of the Harrow gang) spotted her and his name was Steve. He later became known as 'Pikes'. He got this name when a local Asian shopkeeper whose premises had been robbed was asked to describe the miscreant. He said that the person had had 'Pikes on the head mate'. When Steve himself (he was not the robber) later adopted a similar ice cream cone type spiked hairdo, he became 'Pikes'. Anyway, Steve coerced the young and pretty Leda into travelling around with him and his mate Seamus. Tony had by this time got a bit boring and so she had left him behind. They then met up with some other Harrow hippies and wandered about the countryside like troubadours. She and Steve got 'married' on Glastonbury Tor and she dropped her first acid in Cornwall with him, resulting in what was, in her own words a, 'Far out trip.'

They all went to another camp site but got thrown off by the 'straighties' for being too weird, though apparently they hadn't even noticed that they were being disapproved of. Leda was very impressed by her adventures, which included bathing naked in a New Forest stream and eating breakfast by the campfire. For her it was, 'A time of innocence.' And for Steve, who had just been suffering with a severe depression it restored 'butterflies and flowers' to his mind. Aaahh bless.

When they got back Leda two-timed him for a while with Tony before finally plumping for good old 'Pikes.' Pikes was the same age as me and I couldn't have been more thrilled that Leda had got us an 'in' to the Punk crowd at last. He became my style guru and I sat in his garden whilst he put three large bleached blonde streaks into my hair. Grandma hated it, which was always a good sign.

In August, I took David along to a 'Pig Roast' held at Alex and Jayne's in Marsworth. The dog had a great night eating loads of pig fat and was sick and I, naughty person that I am, got into a bit of a preliminary skirmish with Dee. This involved a bit of snogging on a straw bale. I started to carry a bit of a torch for him after that, thinking, 'Oh yes, the strong wise wizard will save me!' Deary me, I just can't help it, it seems. It only served to make things rather embarrassing (for me), when we met on odd occasions and he certainly didn't pursue the matter (if you can call it that) until a bit later.

As well as this, I was of course still mooning over Dennis and sometimes he would speak to me and sometimes he would not. On his birthday early in September, we all went out to celebrate and I had bought him a card with the slogan 'To the object of my affection,' printed upon it. I noticed that he kept it apart from his other cards and put it in his shirt pocket. This I construed as a good sign, though it probably meant that it was destined for the waste bin as soon as he got home. But then bloody John ruined it all by telling him that I was 'mad for the ride'. Honestly, I could have died on the spot and Dennis just said, 'I don't want to screw her life up.'... Eh?

David meanwhile, had become very taken with a young and beautiful boy called Adey who wasn't gay, but you couldn't say he was a hundred per cent straight either. Adey was slim with long pale blond hair. One of those fey types that float about like the seeds of a dandelion clock, just drifting along wherever the breeze may take them. I got on quite well with him and he gave me a present of a pale blue fringed, buckskin jacket. He also played the guitar and wrote songs and we'd often sit and get stoned and have pleasant evenings of harmony and singing in a very Flower Power style man.

Adey was a fan of the wonderful Seventies band, 'Sweet' and David was friendly with a guy called David Priest who just happened to be the brother of none other than Steve Priest, Sweet's bassist (see 1975!). David and David organised for Steve to come out for a drink with us up at The Castle one night so that Adey could meet his hero. Steve Priest turned out to be a really nice bloke and he related an anecdote to me that involved Sweet's drummer Mick Tucker, meeting my Dad at the bar in the Speakeasy one night. Mick was a fan of Dad's so he had approached him and said in a friendly manner, 'Hey Ginger how're you doing?' to which, he reported, my father had replied, 'Minding my own fucking business.'

Steve wanted to know if I thought that this story rang true? And sadly, I had to say that yes, it did. When Steve left us that night he just said, 'Goodbye girls' to Leda and another girl, but he came over and gave me a kiss on the hand and on the lips. Thank you Mr Priest, because that did my ego a world of good and also improved my cred with the onlookers I can tell you. What a great guy.

Autumn was coming on now and I walked back down Vaughan Road from David's in the pouring rain, wearing the buckskin jacket, tight pinstripe jeans and some kitten heeled, red, winkle picker boots I'd saved up for and bought from The Liberated Lady shop in The Kings Road. West Harrow had become 'the village' now to my mind, with its leaf-strewn pavements, its tiny station over hung with beautiful trees and the two large greens of The Gardens, where Solo the dog would go foraging off in the gloom. (All the trees are gone now and the embankment looks rather like Saruman's Orcs have been at it.) As I strolled along I was musing on the fact that Dad was keen to see my sister and brother again and to arrange a meeting seemed like an excellent idea.

Consequently, David, John and I cooked up a plan whereby John would tell Mum he was taking Kofi on holiday and David and I would say we were off somewhere else and as usual, David paid for it all. Leda had already travelled out there with Tony, on a 'just friends' basis. Suddenly, there we all were at the farmhouse in Tuscany, with Dad and Number Two. Dad and Kofi set their drums up on the all but derelict top floor of the house and Leda got out her guitar. It was a moving experience to see the three of them playing together, whilst the complicated rhythms bounced off the bare rafters and onlookers were showered with bits of plaster that had broken loose from the crumbling walls.

Dad went and did a gig down in Rome whilst we were there and a few of us went along. The gig itself took place in a dark underground club, so damp that it had condensation literally dripping off the walls. He played with a bunch of British Northerners who looked like lorry drivers and I kept expecting them to launch into a rendition of the song 'That's Living Alright' at any moment. I had a mild flirtation with the guitarist (well, you have to amuse yourself somehow) and then I got a lift back with a group of Italian teenagers that Dad knew and not one of them spoke a word of English. It was thick fog on the motorway and they were smoking loads of dope and passing a bottle of wine around in the car. I didn't really think that the driver should have been joining in so whole-heartedly with this and as a result I spent the entire journey utterly convinced that this was to be my last night on earth.

But it wasn't. When I got back to the farmhouse, I began to notice that John and Number 2 were doing a lot of flirting. Nonetheless, I honestly believed that as they were both such a couple of tarts that it was only a bit of fun. However, not long after we got back to England, Number 2 flew over and one evening she and John announced that they were in love and going to elope! Well, you could have knocked me down with a feather I can tell you! Meanwhile Dad was left all alone up the mountain with millions of animals to look after.

At the same time as this bombshell was dropped, my little friend Robert reappeared on the scene. He was staying at his parent's place in Ruislip prior to taking up a job as a polo groom in Palm Springs. I took him up to The Castle to let everyone have a good look and then we went back to his place as his parents were away. By now he was seventeen and not a virgin, so consequently I didn't feel quite so bad about finally getting around to doing the deed. I also had a strong presentiment that it was going to be men who eventually did it for him and not girls, so I thought I'd like to have a sample before it was lost to me forever. It wasn't anything like Dennis, but it was very pleasant and we started seeing each other intensely for a few weeks.

Simultaneously, Dad went bonkers about Number 2 and John and so did Mum. The whole thing blew through the roof, then David got jealous of me being with Robert and John said I was neglecting his brother. Tony was phoning Italy doing as much stirring as possible. In fact, he was such a pain over it that we named him Tony 'Wormtongue' after the character in 'The Lord of the Rings' that urges the King of the Rohan lot not to fight. Then the cat had an accident out there and lost part of its tail. So Dad sent it in the post to Number 2's family home and they were so stupid that they really believed that he'd cut it off in a rage! I laughed.

John said he wished he'd never heard the name Baker. Number 2 tried muscling in on my social scene, so I decided that if she wanted the twins then she could have them. She also took Anita with her, mainly because they all became terrified of my mother who was on the warpath. Dad then phoned up saying that he had got an

STD from Number 2 and that John must have it. Of course this was a lie, but just in case it wasn't, I thought I'd have to tell someone as loads of my friends had all been up to things they shouldn't... with John. As a result of this, many other relationships bit the dust and what had once been a fairly cohesive social structure, suddenly collapsed like a house of cards. Not again!

And of course this was also interpreted by dad as being all my fault, in the same way that mum had blamed me for introducing dad to Number 2 (they have no control over their own lives it would seem). Dad moaned on so much about this that I eventually said 'now you know how mum felt'. In reply to this, he wrote me a long letter containing a five Lira coin, saying I was disinherited forever, was a miserable excuse for a human being and should crawl back under the stone I'd come out from. He then ignored me for ages, which I must say came as something of a relief.

Robert and I wisely kept out of the way a bit and stayed over at Mum's most of the time until he left for the States on 15th November. We took a series of photos in the overgrown garden and a melancholy atmosphere prevailed, with the brown and orange leaves hanging in dripping clusters all around us. On November 5th (Guy Fawkes night), Kofi decided he would be man of the house and orchestrate our evening's entertainment. Unfortunately for him, a Roman Candle fell over and accidentally ignited all the rockets, jumping crackers, etc that were in a plastic bag nearby. The bag flew all over the garden at great speed, exploding intermittently, resulting in the quickest firework display ever. Kofi was really pissed off but the rest of us were rendered incoherent with laughter. When Robert left I was very miserable, as I'd really enjoyed having a boyfriend for a while. He wasn't due back until the following April and I knew just as well as everyone else that a hell of a lot could've changed by then, especially in my bloody life.

It was a life that went on in much the same vein. Without David around so much I hung out more with Leda and her new Punk friends, who apart from Steve, were mostly around five years younger than me. Punk had happened to them when they were just ten year-olds at school, yet it seems it had more of an influence on their outlook than on the older ones. However much purists may squawk (and don't they always?) about who, how, where and when were the 'real' Punks, it was after all merely a collection of ideologies that grew and changed over the years. 'Death of the author' and all that. It was primarily an ideal, not a specific set of guidelines. In the words of Josephine Baker talking about her Rainbow Tribe, 'The ideal must be kept alive.'

And this is precisely what the individuals with whom I began to come increasingly into contact with, were doing. I was attracted to both their looks and their clean aggression, which came as a breath of fresh air after the cloying apathy of the hippies. Nevertheless, outcasts are outcasts and the two crowds began to merge. Gradually certain faces crossed the floor like MP's in the House of Commons, only with less acrimony.

As well as Steve and Seamus, I met up with Seamus's then girlfriend, who was a beautiful, reticent and elfin little thing, with a delicate blonde, tiger striped Mohican. Little did I know that this icy vision was in actual fact, 'The Queen of the Scene' herself and the epicentre from which most of the threads of new cool in our local landscape emanated. There was yet another member whom I first espied sitting on the picnic benches outside The Castle and at first, the broad shoulders and shaved head with black spiked fringe and loads of silver earrings made me think it was a geezer, but no, it was 'Big' Lisa. (Soon to become a much-valued friend and supporter, she turned up one day with an electric typewriter and was constantly urging me to write. So this is for her.)

That December, one of my cousins got married in South London and on the hen night, I was the only punkish person cavorting around with the straighties in 'Cinatra's' nightclub in Croydon. I drank twelve scotches, hoped no one would ever notice that I did the Conga and got accosted by a guy who was about four foot tall, which is par for the course in my life. Whilst there, I visited my Nan who'd had a long letter from Number 2, in which she complained that my siblings and I had never supported her. This was the biggest load of bollocks I had ever heard because none of us had ever done anything against her. Except perhaps my brother who had once boiled a large Blue Bottle fly in the kettle (back in Denham) and then made the tea with it. (He always maintained that the fly must have boiled away to nothing, as he never got a glimpse of it in anybody's cup.)

The next week, I stood in Harrow with Sandra one lunchtime, moaning that I had nothing to wear for the actual impending nuptials, so we went to have a look in Miss Selfridge. We spotted an amazing and dramatic, calf length, black jersey dress, with a swinging skirt. It was completely off the shoulder and its long sleeves culminated in fingerless gloves. I immediately fell in love with it and Sandra bought it for me as an early Christmas/birthday present. So Leda and I attended the splicing attired in our own interpretation of wedding clobber. Steve/Pikes my new style advisor, had now dyed my hair black for me, but he left the large bleached strands in place so that I resembled a Badger. I wore the black dress, complete with acres of studs and Leda wore something equally black and scary, complete with pointed and buckled black suede boots.

During the church service, Leda tried a blues version of the hymn 'Praise my soul the King of Heaven' by repeating every line after it had been sung, which I found to be very amusing. We stood for photos outside in the freezing weather and I can't begin to understand why it was that the two of us were placed right at the back. Then we all trooped off for the reception. After the sit down, the only lively tune we could wring out of the DJ was the punk version of 'Nellie the Elephant', so we had to make do with jumping about to that and I then embarked on a long campaign of chatting up a fifteen year-old boy, much to the consternation of his poor mother. Yet he seemed very keen indeed to have his eyes opened to another way of life. I actually thought that we did quite well but when the other daughter (still younger than me), got married the following year, the invitation stipulated that my siblings and I come dressed appropriately or not at all. Seeing as by that time all three of us were sporting Mohicans with shaved sides, there is no way that we could have looked 'normal' in any style of attire whatsoever. We declined that invitation and left them to celebrate their day in peace.

At the very end of 1984, Leda, along with Steve and Seamus had formed a band called The Fen and they did a gig up at The Moonlight Club (once Klooks Kleek where the Graham Bond Organisation & Cream had performed) in West Hampstead. Steve had been part of the now defunct but legendary Harrow combo 'Ritual', a cult band that had come close to hitting the big time. Sadly, I never got to see them, but their mythology lived on, along with that of another successful Harrow band, 'Sunglasses After

Dark'. Even nowadays folks remember the phenomenal talents of the latter's 'Simon the wild violinist', or the imposing figure of Errol, the lead singer of the former, who dominated the stage with a vast black cape slung about his shoulders. He could still be spotted occasionally, early in this century. A quiet and unassuming middle-aged guy, wearing a waxed jacket (with a bit of a cape on it), sitting in the carriage of a Metropolitan Line train.

Wearing the black dress once more, I set off for The Fen gig at this very tiny, dark club. I went along with Seamus, his mate Slimy, Slimy's girlfriend Catherine, and a sweet bloke named J.J. This guy, although only aged about twenty, walked with a stick and had lost most of his hair because he was dying of a brain tumour. We didn't talk about it; we just had a good time with him. At the gig, I noticed a very tall, gangly soul. He looked extremely Marilyn-esque with his long, crimped and unkempt, bleached blond locks tumbling over his shoulders. Oh, how I longed to be properly in their gang, as that I was sure, was where I was going to find all the answers.

My twenty-fourth birthday arrived and it being a Thursday, that meant a mad night dancing to The Bozos up at The Plough. I had invited everyone I could think of from everywhere in order to ensure my chances of getting laid on my birthday, which is one of the golden rules of things you must do. Birthday, Christmas and New Year or you're nowhere. (This could be potentially sad for me as they're all in the same fortnight). Jayne had acquired a knitting machine and had made me a fabulous off the shoulder orange fluffy number that I teamed with a black leather skirt and the inevitable fishnets and high heels. In fact the top was so off the shoulder that I came perilously close to exposing myself on more than one occasion. All my sub-standard admirers flocked around me clamouring for a chance. Dwarfs and trolls a-plenty were waiting for me to get drunk enough to kiss them, but I knew they'd never turn into princes because believe you me I'd already tried.

Then The Wizard made an entrance and he decided to be gracious and turn on the charm. He asked me out to the car for a smoke and as we sat there he said, 'I don't want to marry you or anything, but how about coming back to mine for a shag?'

I looked out of the rain-spattered windscreen and inhaled a large toke. A 183 bus went lumbering by under the neon lights on the Kenton Road and the upstairs passengers stared blankly from its illuminated windows. As per bloody usual, reality collided with fantasyland and momentarily stopped me in my tracks. The Wizard was only Dee trying his luck and I was after all only a goofy semi-punk who was getting older but not wiser. Nevertheless, it was my birthday so I swallowed my disappointment, and said, 'Okay'.

Dee had a beautiful Dutch barge that was moored near the Aylesbury arm of The Grand Union Canal at Marsworth. It could have been a magical and wizardy experience, but I'm sorry to say that it just was not. He had left it too long I guess, and my heart still firmly belonged to Dennis and/or Robert! The next morning the towpath was rimed with frost and Dee dropped me at Wendover station so I could get the train home. I'd left Solo's choke chain on the boat and had to use my own belt for a lead. I must've have presented a right dishevelled sight, staggering along with my fluffy jumper all awry. '*Morning comes the sunrise and I'm driven to my bed / I see that it is empty and there's Devils in my head.*' ...Welcome to 'Four and Twenty'. (CSN&Y)

Even so, scoring the night before had boosted my self-esteem, which was just as well because that very night I encountered Dennis again. In the pub he was with (according to me), an 'ugly blonde,' called Marlene, who was desperately pursuing him as he proceeded to get extremely out of it indeed. The consensus amongst the crowd was that we must all treat him with deference because his beloved ex was planning to marry the pretty singer. He was of course in deep despair (oh, get over it!), but again, everyone was friendly and civilised and never spoke of it outwardly. For some reason, the inebriated Dennis kept looking at me and winking at me and blowing me kisses and then he came and sat on my lap where he knocked over my first drink, and then drank my second one. He was so totally out of it that he kept falling over everywhere, squashing people and dogs as he went.

We all went off to a party and he actually followed *me* into all the rooms for a change but how I wished that he would make up his mind. He kept standing next to me and putting his arm round me and then pelting me with bits of bread and peanuts. I know it doesn't sound very pleasant but it was certainly miles better than him pretending that I didn't exist, which is what he usually did. I decided it was time for me to leave, so I kissed him goodbye and wished him a Merry Christmas. He just stared at me in silence as Marlene held him up hopefully and Leda and I lurched off into the night. Poor Dennis, I felt sorry for him and I still liked him.

Christmas 1984 turned out to be a million times better than the one preceding it. Leda and I spent the big day over at Steve's, where a guy named Trevor (who was one of the hippy lot) joined us. It really was a perfect day. Steve and Trev did the cooking, we watched 'Mary Poppins' were generally silly and we may well have smoked quite a bit of dope, which only added to the hilarity. Leda and I got the hysterical giggles whilst we were washing up and we spent ages lying on the floor crying with laughter and clutching our tea towels for support.

On New Years Eve, we all trooped up to The Castle and Dennis arrived, chatted to me and kissed me! Afterwards we went back to Mum's, where Dennis and I were still together and soon enough we ended up in bed. As usual, I was on cloud one hundred and nine and we did so much talking that I really believed I'd cracked it. He rather obliquely asked me what I thought our chances were and ever the optimist I replied, 'Good.' He said he was sorry that he'd been so awful to me, but had felt it necessary because I had, 'Got too close.' This is a line he used to me again as an explanation for this behaviour about seven years later in The King's Head one night. On that occasion he was trying to talk me out of getting married. It is quite frankly the lamest excuse I have ever heard and it doesn't really mean anything. The shame of it all is that I think in reality we could have had quite a good relationship because Dennis later went on to do an English degree as I did, and so intellectually there must have been something more in his head than he ever let on about. But Dennis never even tried to have a decent conversation with me; perhaps he didn't think girls were capable of it? Never mind. As the bells rang and father time handed us the wonderful 1985, I believed he was mine and there can have been no better feeling however fleeting it may have been.

... To be continued.